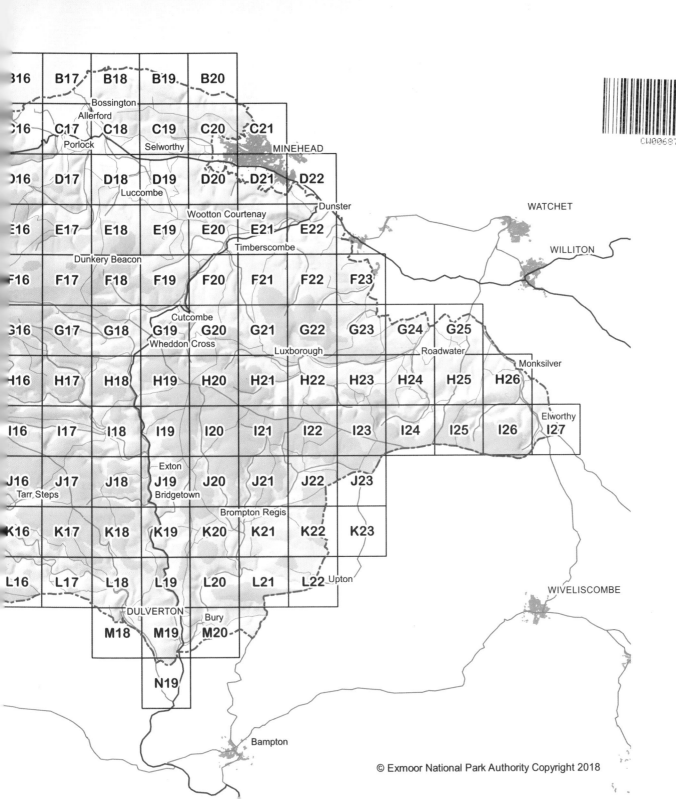

© Exmoor National Park Authority Copyright 2018

CW00687643

Exploring Exmoor from Square One

A Guide to Every Grid Square of the National Park

Nigel Stone

HALSGROVE

First published in Great Britain in 2019

British Library Cataloguing-in-Publication Data
A CIP record for this title is available from the British Library

ISBN 978 0 85704 338 2

Royalties from the sales of this book are to be donated to The Exmoor Trust. The Trust aims to support the local community and conserve and enhance for the public benefit the Exmoor area and to encourage appreciation of all aspects of its historical, physical and cultural environment.

HALSGROVE
Halsgrove House,
Ryelands Business Park, Bagley Road,
Wellington, Somerset TA21 9PZ
Tel: 01823 653777   Fax: 01823 216796
email: sales@halsgrove.com

Part of the Halsgrove group of companies
Information on all Halsgrove titles is available at:
www.halsgrove.com

Printed in India by Parksons Graphics

C18 *Cottage in Bossington.*

Stag roaring.

F12 *Little Exe.*

Introduction

An explorer of Exmoor National Park is faced with huge variety at every turn. From the high, wet grass moors with their areas of blanket bog; through long wooded valleys with clear fast-flowing rivers; across the drier coastal heather-clad heaths, to a spectacular coast with some of the highest sea cliffs in England and saltmarsh where Porlock Vale meets the sea. As the scenery changes, so does the flora and wildlife. Exmoor is notable for the unique Exmoor Pony; the wild red deer, and many species now rare elsewhere in Britain such as the High Brown and Heath Fritillary butterflies.

It is thought that the area we know as Exmoor today began to take shape around 25 million years ago when tectonic forces lifted a plateau composed largely of Devonian sandstones and slates from the surrounding landscape. Subsequent erosion by wind, rain, snow and ice has left the rounded hills, deep valleys and high sea cliffs that make Exmoor one of the finest landscapes in Britain. This origin also means that Exmoor is very different in character from the granite upland landscapes of Dartmoor and Bodmin Moor that lie to the south and west with their granite tors, boulders and outcrops.

Exmoor's varied landscape contains traces of habitation by people over at least 8000 years, from nomadic Mesolithic hunter gatherer campsites to Bronze Age and Iron Age settlements. As settlement intensified, people shaped the landscape through farming to provide the intricate patterns of moors, woods and fields with the distinctive high stone-faced banks topped by hedges predominantly of beech. Mining, quarrying and industry have also left their mark.

The result is a landscape of beauty and interest, and the aim of this book is to convey something of the variety and richness that rewards any time spent exploring Exmoor National Park. It is a celebration of a special place where I have had the privilege to live and work for the past nineteen years.

B08 *A Valley of Rocks goat taking in the view!*

The Exmoor 'Photomap'

The origins of this book lie in a project between 2014 and 2017 to take a photograph in each kilometre square on the Exmoor Ordnance Survey map. Undertaking the project was a voyage of discovery. I thought I knew Exmoor quite well but the project took me to many new locations across the National Park and demonstrated the considerable variety and areas of interest that exist on Exmoor. The aim of the book has been to try and capture something of this variety and, hopefully, to help stimulate a curiosity and encouragement to discover more of Exmoor for yourself.

A map-based approach has been retained in this book but, rather than referring to individual grid squares (there are more than 650), a grid of 2km x 2km squares has been used to provide the structure. The map can be found inside the front and back covers with a label for each square comprising a letter for the row and a number for the column, e.g. A10; B02; B03 etc. The individual map squares are covered in order through book which can be dipped-into and browsed as well as read from front to back.

To look for specific locations, you can use the map on the inside covers as a guide. The Ordnance Survey 1:25,000 scale. Explorer map for Exmoor – OL9 – can be used to provide more detail on the locations in the photographs.

As well as photographs for locations across the National Park, the book includes a number of pages dedicated to specific topics, as follows:

Topic:	Page:
Heddon's Rare Fritillary Butterflies	12
Mire Restoration	65
Exmoor's Dark Skies	66
Exmoor's Red Deer	72
The Small Fritillary Butterflies	91
Cobweb in Dew	93
Exmoor Ponies	130
References and Further Reading	176

Author's Acknowledgements

I would like to thank those who read through copies of the manuscript, particularly Rob Wilson-North and Tim Gunhouse. Thanks also to Matt Sully, Exmoor National Park Authority, who kindly produced the map that is key to the structure and use of this book, and to Steven Pugsley and Karen Binaccioni at Halsgrove for seeing the book from outline through to the finished product.

Ultimately, most thanks are due to those people, past and present, who, through their hard work and passion, have made Exmoor the wonderful place that it is today.

Perhaps curiosity can apply to sheep as well as cats?

A10 Butter Hill and Foreland Point

The Hangman Grit cliffs at Butter Hill, Countisbury provide a dramatic scene from the coast road above Lynmouth. Foreland Point sits on the most northerly point of Devon and Exmoor, overlooking the Bristol Channel and Wales beyond.

A10 *The remains of two gun emplacements are visible from the coast path on the northern slopes of Wind Hill. With good vantage over the Bristol Channel, the remains are thought to date from the First World War. A small building on the site might have been a shelter or ammunition store.*

A10 *Foreland Point lighthouse was constructed in 1900 and was automated in 1994. The lighthouse keepers' cottage is owned by The National Trust and used as a holiday let.*

A10 *The slopes of Butter Hill looking towards Foreland Point. The red scars mark the latest of the regular rockfalls.*

B02 Little Hangman and Hangman Point

The Exmoor coast stretches some 55 kilometres (34 miles) from Combe Martin to Minehead. Much of the coast is formed by high cliffs, with occasional small coves where rivers and streams enter the sea. Little Hangman provides the most westerly high point at 218 metres.

A detailed survey of aerial photographs of Exmoor has revealed the presence of a substantial earthwork encircling the hill top of Little Hangman.[8]

This is thought to be the remains of a 'Tor Enclosure' dating from the late Neolithic or early Bronze Age around 4000 years ago. Similar sites have been recorded on Bodmin Moor in Cornwall and Dartmoor in Devon, but were previously unknown on Exmoor.

The precise function of Tor Enclosures is not certain but they are likely to reflect the most significant features in the landscape for people at the time [1].

B02 *Looking west from the coast path towards Little Hangman.*

B03 and B04
Great Hangman

Great Hangman is the highest point on the Exmoor coast at 318 metres and the sea cliffs on its northern face are the highest in England.

B04 *The Mare and Colt are a distinctive pair of rocks below Holdstone Down.*

B03 *Looking east towards the high point of Great Hangman with Blackstone Point below and Highveer Point in the distance.*

B05 Trentishoe

Trentishoe is a small settlement on high ground between Heddon valley and sea cliffs above the Bristol Channel. The small church dates from the fifteenth century.

B05 Trentishoe sits on a 240-metre-high headland rising from the Bristol Channel.

B05 *Trentishoe Church.*

B05 Heddon's Mouth Cleave and Heddon's Mouth

The wooded Heddon valley leads to a small, secluded cove at Heddon's Mouth. Its seclusion made the cove ideal for smugglers and there are accounts of German U-boats using the cove in the Second World War to land and provide a rest break for the crew[2]. Several boats have been lost on the rocks at Highveer Point to the west of the cove with the largest known wreck being of the *Alethea*, an English cutter lost in 1906.[1]

[Facing page]
B05 *Heddon's Mouth.*

B05 *Highveer rocks revealed at low tide.*

B05 *Remains of a lime kiln at Heddon's Mouth.*

B05 *Heddon's Mouth Cleave.*

Heddon's Rare Fritillary Butterflies

Bracken slopes above the Heddon valley woodland provide one of the last strongholds in Britain for the very rare High Brown Fritillary butterfly. These large and active butterflies can be seen on the wing from mid-June until early August. Active management is needed to keep conditions just right for the butterfly. Too little bracken and the violets that provide food for the caterpillars are overgrown by grasses, too much and bracken blocks out the warm spring sunshine needed for the caterpillars to grow successfully. In the past, the ideal conditions would have been maintained by grazing cattle and ponies.

High Brown Fritillary feeding on nectar from a bramble flower.

High Brown Fritillary on bracken showing the distinctive underside wing markings with a row of blurred red/brown spots with silver centres.

The more common Dark Green and Silver-washed Fritillary butterflies are of a similar size and can be confused with the High Brown Fritillary. Dark Green Fritillaries have a greenish hue to the undersides of the hind wings with large silver spots. They occur throughout Britain. The Silver-washed Fritillary has silver streaks on the underside of its wings rather than silvery spots as in the other larger Fritillary species. This butterfly is found mainly in southern England.

Two smaller species of fritillary butterfly can also be found on Exmoor and are described on page 91.

Silver-washed Fritillary showing the underside of the wings with the distinctive silvery streaks.

Dark Green Fritillary – note the silver spots but no red/brown eye spots on the underside of the hind wings.

B06 and B07 **Martinhoe, North Devon Coast and Lee Abbey**

High cliffs continue between Highveer Point at Heddon's Mouth and Woody Bay, offering views along the North Devon coast.

Inland is the small settlement of Martinhoe and the parish church of St Martin, which was completed in a form recognisable today at the end of the eleventh century. The rood screen dates to the fifteenth century.[1]

Heading east from Heddon valley, further beaches can be accessed at Woody Bay and Lee Bay. The latter falls within the grounds of Lee Abbey. The area was given to the Cistercian Abbots of Forde Abbey in Somerset in 1199, but it is not thought that the Cistercians undertook any large-scale development on the site. The name 'Lee Abbey' was bestowed by the owner following a large-scale extension of the house in 1850 in the neo gothic style. The Tower Lodge and Duty Point Tower were developed shortly afterwards as part of the romantic landscape gardens around the house.

B07 *The Abbey was originally a private home and now provides the home for a Christian retreat.*

B06 *View east from the coast path showing West Woody Bay Wood; the rock arch of Wringapeak; Crock Point; Duty Point below Lee Abbey; Castle Rock and Rugged Jack in the Valley of Rocks, and a distant Foreland Point beyond Lynmouth.*

B08 Valley of Rocks

The Valley of Rocks is a dry valley that runs parallel to the coast west of Lynton. The process by which it was formed is a mystery. One theory suggests that cliffs to the north of the current coastline diverted the River Lyn westwards down what is now the Valley of Rocks. According to this theory, subsequent erosion of these sea cliffs led to the River Lyn breaking through at Lynmouth and leaving Valley of Rocks high and dry. An alternative theory suggests that ice sheets reached the Exmoor coast during one of the glacial periods to block the River Lyn and form a lake which drained through the Valley of Rocks. When the ice sheet retreated, the river resumed its former course to the sea at Lynmouth.

However it was formed, the valley has been a popular attraction for centuries. In 1797, Samuel Taylor Coleridge and William Wordsworth visited the valley together and decided to write a prose tale set there called "The Wanderings of Cain", though it was never completed. The poet Robert Southey was a visitor in August 1799, describing it as *"covered with huge stones … the very bones and skeletons of the earth; rock reeling upon rock, stone piled upon stone, a huge terrific mass."*[2]

B08 *Castle Rock in the late evening sunshine.*

[Facing page]
B08 *Sunset from Wringcliff Bay at the foot of Castle Rock.*

B08 *Valley of Rocks from Hollerday Hill, with Duty Point Tower and Wringapeak just visible and Highveer Point in the distance.*

B09 Lynmouth

East and West Lyn Rivers meet shortly before entering the sea at Lynmouth. The wide delta of large stones and boulders is testament to the severe floods that can affect the Lyn catchment during high rainfall. Most notoriously on Friday 15 August 1952, when around 9 inches (23 cm) of rain fell on the high ground of Exmoor Forest. This led to huge floods in all of Exmoor's rivers and to catastrophic damage as the East Lyn and West Lyn Rivers converged on Lynmouth. Ninety-three buildings in Lynmouth were destroyed or had to be demolished and 34 people lost their lives that night. It took many months to repair the damage and the river channels are now considerably larger as a precaution against any future flood of a similar scale.

B09 *The Lyn River and Lynmouth harbour. The channel for the Lyn River has been considerably widened since the catastrophic floods in August 1952.*

B09 Beach at Lynmouth and Sillery Sands

To the east of Lynmouth the land falls steeply from Wind Hill to the shore. Venturing beyond the aptly named 'Point Perilous' is only possible at very low tides and there is a danger of getting cut off as the tide comes in so care needs to be taken to know the tide times. The rocks on the shore nearest Lynmouth are part of the same 'Lynton Formation' as at Valley of Rocks and are the oldest on Exmoor having been laid down some 400 million years ago. Around a kilometre east from Point Perilous there is a big gully that marks a fault between the older rocks and the Hangman Sandstone of Butter Hill and Foreland Point **(A10)**.

B09 *Large rock outcrops are a dramatic feature of the shore east of Lynmouth.*

B09 *Looking back to Lynmouth from the beach.*

B09 *View from Sillery Sands to Lynmouth. Sillery Sands should only be accessed for a very short time at very low tides to allow return before getting cut off by the rising tide.*

B09 *Access to steps at Sillery Sands is no longer possible from the coast path following coastal erosion and a series of rock falls.*

B10 Countisbury

Countisbury is a small settlement on the high ridge followed by the A39 from Lynmouth to Porlock. To the west lies the Iron Age 'promontory fort' at Wind Hill. It is the largest promontory fort in England with impressive embankments to augment the natural stronghold. Wind Hill is considered a possible location for the Battle of Cynuit in 878 AD, when Odda, Ealdorman of Devon, led an Anglo-Saxon force to defeat a Viking army led by Ubba, brother of Ivar the Boneless and Halfdan Ragnarsson. Ubba was killed in the battle and the capture by Odda of the 'Hrefn', the Raven banner, was recorded in the Anglo-Saxon Chronicle.[1,2]

B10 *Wind Hill viewed from Countisbury showing the Iron Age Promontory Fort and possible site of the Battle of Cynuit in 878.*

B10 *Myrtleberry North Iron Age Camp on a promontory in the East Lyn valley taken from South Hill Common, Countisbury.*

B11 Desolate to Brendon

The high ridge continues east from Countisbury with the Bristol Channel to the north and East Lyn valley to the south. The small nineteenth-century farmstead named 'Desolate' reflects the remoteness of the coast as does 'Desolation Point' below Wingate Combe.

B11 *Looking over Desolate to The Foreland from the top of Wingate Combe.*

Young trout and salmon from the East Lyn with parr markings. The salmon (below) can be distinguished by its more streamlined shape, more deeply forked tail and the longer pectoral fins on the side behind the gills.

B11 *Late seventeenth or early eighteenth century packhorse bridge at Brendon over the East Lyn River.*

Inland, the ridge is bounded by the East Lyn and the village of Brendon alongside the river. The parish church of St Brendan is roughly 2 miles (3 km) to the west **(C10)**.

The East Lyn River receives little pollution and its clear water provides a home for trout and salmon. Periodic monitoring by the Environment Agency is undertaken to assess the stocks of young fish.

B11 *Electrofishing at Brendon using an electric current to temporarily stun the fish so they can be counted and measured before being allowed to recover and returned to the river.*

B12 *Panoramic view of Old Burrow Roman fortlet looking east.*

B12 County Gate and Glenthorne

County Gate marks the boundary between Somerset and Devon. Just to the north is Old Burrow Hill, the site of a Roman fortlet. The fortlet was probably built in around 50AD and is thought to have been occupied only for a short time before the garrison was moved westwards to a similar lookout further along the coast at Martinhoe **(B06)**.

A re-enactment of life in the Roman fortlet at Old Burrow was held at an event in 2004.

B12 *Sisters Fountain is below County Gate. The stone structure surrounds a spring head and has a stone cross above. It dates from the early nineteenth century and is situated on the hillside above Glenthorne, the house built for the Revd W. S. Halliday and begun in 1829.*

B13 and B14 Remote Coast and Hanging Coastal Woods

B13 *The beach at Glenthorne is accessible by a steep path from County Gate.*

Steep wooded cliffs overlook the Bristol Channel between Lynmouth and Porlock Weir. The woods east of Glenthorne form the longest stretch of hanging coastal woodland in England. Hanging is the name given to woodlands on a steep slope. A small number of very steep paths provide access to secluded pebble beaches.

B14 *Holmer's Combe heading down to Culbone Wood.*

B13 *A small cave in the cliffs below Glenthorne. Here the Devonian Hangman Sandstone rocks have been tilted to nearly vertical.*

B15 Culbone Church and Ashley Combe

Dedicated to the Welsh saint Beuno, the secluded and picturesque Culbone church is thought to be the smallest parish church in England and seats about 30 people. The church is probably Anglo-Saxon in origin and is mentioned in the Domesday Book. The tall nave and bowl font are Saxon features and the small window in the north wall carved from a single block of stone is probably also Saxon. The porch is thirteenth century and the nave is late fifteenth century, while the windows and roof were refurbished in around 1810. The small spire was added in 1888.[1]

B15 *Culbone Church.*

Ashley Combe was built in 1799 as a hunting lodge. It was improved at great expense by Lord King in 1835 for the honeymoon when William King (and later 1st Earl of Lovelace) married Augusta Ada Byron, the only legitimate child of the poet Lord Byron and his wife, Annabella Milbanke. Ada Lovelace had inherited her mother's interest in mathematics and was very active in intellectual London Society. In particular, she established a working relationship with Charles Babbage, the inventor of the 'Difference Engine', and is credited with having set the ground for future developments in computing.[24]

Little now remains of Ashley Combe House although some of the garden features can still be seen including a series of small tunnels that form part of the route of the South West Coast Path at Worthy.

B15 *Tunnel used by the South West Coast Path at Worthy Combe is a former garden feature from Ashley Combe House.*

B15 *Worthy Toll Road runs south west from Porlock Weir to the Culbone Inn within the Ashley Combe estate. The very distinctive Ashley Combe Lodge provides the easterly entrance to the toll road.*

B16 Porlock Weir harbour

The small harbour at Porlock Weir has existed for more than a thousand years. Famously, the harbour provided the launching point on 12 January 1899 when *Louisa*, the Lynmouth lifeboat, set out to rescue the crew of the *Forest Hall* sailing ship. A severe gale meant it was not possible to launch at Lynmouth so the decision was made to haul the 10-tonne lifeboat from Lynmouth to the safer launching point at Porlock Weir – a distance of 15 miles (24 km) and including the extremely steep 1 in 4 (25%) hills at Countisbury and Porlock.

After the 11-hour haul across Exmoor, the lifeboat was launched at 06.30 on 13 January and the crew had to row for an hour in the storm to reach the stricken vessel anchored off Hurlestone Point.

The lifeboat held station until daybreak when two tugs arrived and towed the ship across the Bristol Channel to Barry. The *Louisa* and crew accompanied the crossing in case of further problems and were towed back to Lynmouth by a steam ship once the *Forest Hall* was safely in port.

B16 *The dock at Porlock Weir possibly dates back to the fifteenth century. It was improved in the early nineteenth century by installation of gates that enabled water to be retained at low tide for loading and unloading boats. At one time, vessels of up to 100 tons came into Porlock Weir and there was a flourishing trade with South Wales, bringing in coal, limestone and cement and exporting agricultural produce, tan bark, charcoal and pit props.[1]*

B16 *High tide at Porlock Weir. The harbour is now mainly used by leisure craft.*

B17 Bossington Beach and Hurlestone Point

B17 *The breach in the shingle ridge that was caused by the storm in October 1996.*

B17 *At very high Spring tides, the whole area of saltmarsh is inundated.*

From Porlock Weir, a long shingle ridge extends eastwards in an arc along the shoreline becoming progressively more massive as pebbles and shingle pile up towards the headland at Hurlestone Point. The pebbles are being moved from west to east by waves and currents in a process known as longshore drift. Following a breach in the ridge caused by a storm in October 1996, the controversial decision was made to allow natural processes to take place rather than rebuild the ridge artificially. Since then, a salt marsh has developed on land that is inundated at high tides.

B17 *Bossington beach at sunset showing the extent of the shingle ridge with Bossington Hill in the background and the saltmarsh that has formed since the breach in 1996.*

B17 *Breaches of the shingle ridge are a regular occurrence during severe weather. A particularly spectacular breach took place on 30 April 2012, when flooding of the River Aller built up behind the ridge and burst through to displace thousands of tons of shingle. Within a year, much of the shingle had been moved back by natural tidal movements and the River Aller now drains through the shingle ridge as it did before.*

Archaeological remains on this section of the shingle ridge include a large nineteenth century lime kiln and remains of the Second World War defences including concrete and stone pillboxes.

B17 *View through the gun slit of one of the Second World War 'pillbox' defences.*

B17 *Nineteenth-century lime kiln on Bossington Beach.*

From Hurlestone Point eastwards, Devonian sandstones form a ridge from Bossington Hill and Selworthy Beacon to North Hill above Minehead. Steep valleys lead down to the Bristol Channel in several places.

[Left] **B18** *Henners Combe leading down to Selworthy Sands.*

B18 *Selworthy Sands exposed at low tide. It looks inviting but access is difficult and hazardous!*

B19 *Furzebury Break, an Iron Age oval enclosure or hillfort above Grexy Combe.*

The heathland on North Hill provides a good habitat for the Dartford Warbler. Unusually for a warbler, the Dartford Warbler is resident all year round rather than migrating south for the winter. This can lead to big drops in population in hard winters.

B20 *Dartford Warbler at North Hill.*

Lester Point at Combe Martin is the most westerly point of Exmoor National Park.

C02 **Knap Down, West Challacombe and Silver Mines, Combe Martin**

Combe Martin grew up along the valley of the River Umber that runs through the Ilfracombe slate rocks. This rock formation includes significant beds of limestone and umber is a red mineral pigment found in rotted limestone[3]. North of Combe Martin, the Ilfracombe Slates are bounded by the harder Hangman Sandstones that form the high sea cliffs of Little and Great Hangman **(B02** and **B03)**.

The Ilfracombe Slate rocks around Combe Martin contain a variety of minerals including deposits of galena which is a lead ore that often contains significant amounts of silver. Records indicate mining from the late thirteenth century when, in 1293 (the rein of Edward I), 337 Derbyshire men were moved south to work the Combe Martin mines.[3] Items in the Crown Jewels are made from Combe Martin silver and a large part of the war expenses of Edward III and Henry V were paid for by the sale of silver mined here.[2]

C02 *Ivy-clad ruins of the engine house of Knap Down Silver Mine, Combe Martin.*

C02 *View to Little Hangman from Knap Down.*

C03 *Cairn and trig point on Holdstone Down (349 metres). The remains of three Bronze Age cairns are situated at the top of Holdstone Hill.*

C04 *Trentishoe Down from Tattiscombe.*

C05 *Heale is a small group of farmsteads on a promontory above the River Heddon. Several of the farms have ancient origins.*

C05 *Cascades on the River Heddon below Heale Down.*

C06 *Small blue door at Kittitoe – for Hobbits maybe?*

C07 *Woody Bay station with the engine 'Isaac'. Isaac was built in 1953 for a mining company in South Africa and its restoration was completed in 2012. Woody Bay station is on the former narrow-gauge railway line between Barnstaple and Lynton. The original railway was opened in May 1898 but was relatively short-lived and closed in September 1935.*

C09 *The two standing stones on Lyn Down are relatively large for Exmoor with the tallest at 2.1m. Unfortunately, they have been moved from their original locations and little is known of their origins.*

C08 *Remains of a railway bridge at New Mill that was formerly part of the Lynton & Barnstaple Railway route.*

[Facing page] **C06** *View to Trentishoe Down from Killington.*

C10 *St Brendan's church is around 2 miles from Brendon with Butter Hill and Countisbury Common in the background. St Brendan's church was built in 1738, with much restoration and rebuilding in the nineteenth century. It replaced a church of twelfth-century foundation at Cheriton and the twelfth-century font may have come from there.[1]*

C10 *The East Lyn River at Rockford.*

C11 Tippacott Ridge, Brendon Common

C11 *View of the northern area of Brendon Common taken from Tippacott Ridge.*

Brendon Common is managed by a Commons Council that was established in 2014. The council is elected for a period of two years by the membership comprising the landowner and people entitled to graze animals on the common.

C11 *Typically, field boundaries on Exmoor are earth banks protected by stone facings, often but not always with a beech hedge on top. This picture of a repaired bank on Easter Lane, Brendon, taken in 2009, demonstrates the skill employed in bank construction.*

C12 Badgworthy Water and Malmsmead

Brendon Common is bounded in the east by Badgworthy Water (pronounced "Badgery"). The river also forms the boundary between Devon and Somerset counties.

C12 *Badgworthy Water south of Cloud Farm. Badgworthy is often regarded as the inspiration for the romantic novel* Lorna Doone: A Romance of Exmoor *written by the Reverend R. D. Blackmore and published in 1869. After a faltering start, sales increased and the novel has been popular ever since. While not intended to be historically accurate, the story is often spoken of as if it was factual!*

C12 *The seventeenth-century packhorse bridge at Malmsmead provides the only vehicular crossing of Badgworthy Water. After a short distance north of Malmsmead, the river joins Oare Water to form the East Lyn that flows on to the sea at Lynmouth.*

C13 Oare

The church of St Mary in Oare is of medieval origin but much restored and altered, containing eighteenth-century features such as box pews, a readers' desk and a pulpit.[1] The grandfather of *Lorna Doone* author, R.D. Blackmore, was Rector here (1809-42) and the church is the setting for the fictional wedding in the novel of Lorna Doone to John Ridd (see **C12**).

North Common is a small block of moorland above Oare Water. As well as sheep and cattle, Exmoor ponies are grazed on the common. Exmoor ponies are rounded up once a year in the autumn to check their health and ensure that the foals meet the breed standard. Any foals that are destined to be sold are removed and the remainder of the herd is then allowed to return to the moor. (For more on Exmoor Ponies, see page 130.)

C13 *Ponies from North Common in the pens for their annual check.*

C13 *Oare church from Deddy Combe.*

C14 *Robber's Bridge provides a narrow crossing over Weir Water. The awkward angle of the bridge, plus less-than-perfect driving, means that the low parapet is regularly damaged by vehicles!*

C14 **Robber's Bridge and Weir Water**

The secluded valley of Weir Water above Robber's Bridge provided the location for a medieval farmstead known as Weirwood. Weirwood is shown as an inhabited farmstead on the 1st Edition Ordnance Survey map of 1890, and so must have been abandoned after this date.[1]

C14 *Weir Water rises just north of Lucott Cross and drains the moors at Porlock Allotment, Mill Hill and the west side of Porlock Common.*

C15 **Pittcombe Head and Porlock Common**

The narrow road from Robber's Bridge leads up to Oare Post and Pittcombe Head at the westerly end of Porlock Common.

C15 *Originally, Automobile Association (AA) boxes contained an emergency phone and equipment for use by AA members requiring assistance. Some 862 boxes were installed around the country up until the early 1960s, but now only 19 remain.*

C15 *Exmoor Ponies on Porlock Common with Porlock Marsh, Hurlestone Point and the Bristol Channel in the background.*

C15 *Porlock Common lies to the east of Pittcombe Head and is still managed as common land. The 'Whit Stones' are two relatively large stones (for Exmoor) that form a significant feature on the common. Little is known of their origins although it has been suggested that they might be the remains of a prehistoric burial chamber.*

C15 *A tired competitor completing the ascent of New Road at Pittcombe Head. New Road is a toll road constructed in the 1840s from Porlock as a scenic route rather than an alternative to the main road at Porlock Hill. At around 4.5 miles (7 km) the route follows a gentler gradient than Porlock Hill but still provides a stern test for cyclists during the annual Porlock Hill Climb event.*

C16 Porlock Beach and Porlock Weir 'Tin Tabernacle'

Porlock Beach holds a good deal of archaeological interest including the remains of a sunken forest that grew in the area before sea levels rose as the ice sheets retreated at the end of the last Ice Age. The peat layers within the forest have yielded shaped flints left by people using the area in the Mesolithic and Neolithic periods (around 11,600 to 4500 years ago).

Following the erosion of the beach during a major storm in October 1996, the remains of the skeleton of a giant Aurochs were discovered in beach sediments. The Aurochs is a species of giant ox and tests indicate that the animal at Porlock was an adult bull at least ten years old that lived sometime between 3700 and 3450 years ago (early Bronze Age). Aurochs are thought to have become extinct in Britain around 3000 years ago during the late Bronze Age.

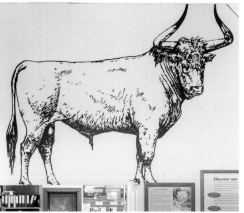

C16 *The Porlock remains of the Porlock Aurochs are on display at the Porlock Visitor Centre*

[Right] **C16** *In a raised position on the small road from Porlock Weir to West Porlock is St Nicholas church, a "tin tabernacle" probably dating from the late nineteenth century, and little altered. Prefabricated structures made of corrugated iron provided a relatively economical means of building in the latter part of the nineteenth and early part of the twentieth centuries. Many manufacturers produced catalogues including chapels of various sizes.*

C16 *The effects of winter storms can be seen at Porlock Beach where the shingle has been pushed back beyond a large oak tree that had been above the shingle in 2013.*

C17 Porlock

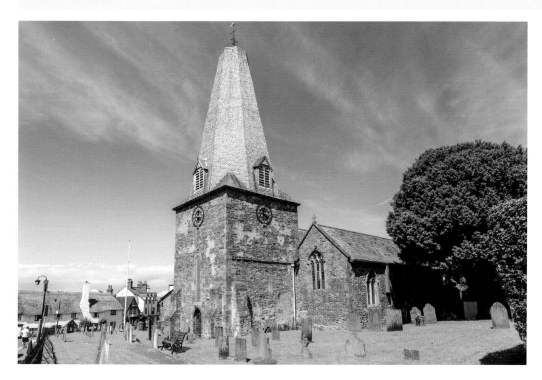

C17 *Porlock church, dedicated to St Dubricius, was probably built about 1120 to commemorate the removal of the saint's remains from the Isle of Bardsey to Llandaff. The east tower and wooden framework of the spire date from the early thirteenth century and there are remains of thirteenth-century work in the south aisle wall. The arcade dates from around 1400 and the porch and nave windows are fifteenth century. A fragment of a Saxon cross-shaft with interlaced ornament is preserved in the church.*[1]

Porlock's history can be traced back at least as far as the Anglo-Saxons. It is referred to as Portloc in the Domesday Book, a name derived from the Old English 'port' and 'loca' meaning the enclosed port. There is evidence of Danish raids in the mid 800s and early 900s. Porlock was destroyed by Harold (later King Harold of the Battle of Hastings) in 1052 when he defeated an army from Somerset and Devon. The battle occurred because Algar, brother of Hereward the Wake and son of Leofric, Earl of Mercia, was Lord of the Manor and opposed Godwin, Harold's father, who held manors inland, including Dulverton.[1]

C17 *Doverhay, at the eastern end of Porlock, was a separate manor and fell within the adjoining Luccombe parish until 1930. Dovery Manor is now a local heritage museum.*

C18 and C19 **Allerford, Selworthy and the Holnicote Estate**

The Holnicote estate lies to the east of Porlock and has a scatter of small and picturesque settlements, many of which have ancient roots, such as those at Bossington, Allerford and Selworthy. Holnicote (pronounced Hunnicot) is referred to as Hunnecota in the Domesday Book, thought to mean the cottage of a person named 'Hun'.

The estate was in the Acland family for nearly 200 years having been acquired in 1745 through marriage and gifted to the National Trust in 1934 – see page 89. The Holnicote estate includes many memorials to the Acland family.

C18 To the east of the same car park is a stone-built shelter built in 1878 in memory of Thomas Dyke Acland (1787-1871). Recesses include poems by Heber and Keble extolling the beauty of the countryside. Thomas Dyke Acland holds an important place in the history of the 'Picturesque' movement for his improvement of the Holnicote estate, particularly notable being the cottages around Selworthy Green.

C18 Selworthy Cross was erected in memory of Thomas Dyke Acland (1809-1896). It is 250 metres south west of the car park at the end of the road near Selworthy Beacon in a small clearing in the surrounding woodland.

C18 South from the memorial shelter lies a wooden shelter built in around 1879 for Gertrude, wife of Sir Charles Thomas Dyke Acland (12th Baronet), presumably as a location for picnicking. The picture was taken in early February 2009 after heavy snow.

Selworthy is named Selewrda in the Domesday Book meaning enclosure near sallows or willows.[4] In 1828, it was rebuilt by Sir Thomas Acland as a model village to provide housing for the aged and infirm of the Holnicote estate.[2]

C19 *On the hill above Selworthy village is the whitewashed fifteenth-century church of All Saints, with a fourteenth-century tower, here photographed in February 2009.*

C18 *Cottages on Selworthy Green.*

C18 *The much-photographed medieval packhorse bridge in Allerford.*

C18 *Buddle Hill may owe its name to the West Somerset dialect word – to buddle, meaning to bury in mud!*

C20 and C21 **North Hill, Minehead**

In places along the ridge from Bossington Hill to Selworthy Beacon and North Hill, traces can still be seen of the use of the area as a tank training ground in the Second World War. Tanks would fire from one of three triangular tracks set out at intervals along the ridge. Each of the triangular tracks had a moving target on the seaward side[1].

C20 *View of the former tank servicing area. The fencing and triangular concrete blocks are recent additions.*

C20 *The operations block of the Second World War radar station is well preserved, although the antenna has been removed.*

As well as the tank grounds, North Hill was also the site for a radar station that formed part of a chain of coastal defence stations. The operations block is still standing and the mounts for the radar antenna are visible on the roof.

C20 *A reconstruction drawing of the radar station as it might have looked with its roof-mounted antenna. (Copyright ENPA)*

D05 *View from above Voley.*

D04 and D05 **Dean and Voley**

The majority of landscape in this area is cultivated fields accessed via narrow lanes and with few rights of way. Dean Wood and Cowley Wood are the most significant features.

D04 *Dean Wood taken from Voley. Dean is from the Old English 'denu' and means valley while Voley is probably a derivation of 'foley', a local word for fern clearing.*

D06 *A panorama of Parracombe taken from Rowley Down to the south. All Saints church to the left of centre was built in 1878 to replace the original St Petrock's parish church to the east in Churchtown leaving the latter happily 'unrestored'! Heddon Hall is prominent in the centre of the picture. It is now a private house but was originally built as a Rectory in the 1820s.*

Parracombe is situated on the convergence of several narrow lanes that meet in a steep valley. There is no clear definition of the source of the name of the village which is called Pedracomba in the Domesday Book (1086). It may derive from the Old English 'pearr' or 'enclosure'. The *Oxford Dictionary of Place Names* refers to 'peddera cumb', also Old English, meaning 'the pedlars valley'. Other sources suggest that it is a corruption of 'Petrock's Combe' based on the dedication of the original parish church at Churchtown – thought to be the original settlement. St Petrock is better known as a Cornish saint, although, on Exmoor, Timberscombe church is also dedicated to him **(E20)**.

The church of St Petrock may have been founded as early as 525AD but the earliest fabric of the current building is in the tower which is dated to about 1180. The chancel and probably most of the tower date to the thirteenth century. The nave, south aisle and south porch are late fifteenth or early sixteenth century in date. In 1879 there were worries about the stability of the building and it was proposed to demolish the church and build a replacement on the site. However, protests led by John Ruskin, who donated £10, led to the preservation of the church and the construction of a new one further west in the village[1].

D06 *St Petrock's church, Churchtown escaped 'restoration' in the nineteenth century.*

D06 *Interior of St Petrock's church with box pews, Georgian pulpit and a screen with a wooden tympanum above it which all date from the eighteenth century.*

Holwell Castle is a classic example of a Norman motte-and-bailey castle and would originally have had timber defences on the earthworks. It is likely to have been built either during the Norman conquest or in the civil war of the twelfth century. Its location suggests that it was built to dominate Parracombe and its river crossing. Its name derives from a small spring nearby that may once have been considered a holy well although there is no evidence of any former structures at the spring site. Unlike many similar motte-and-bailey castles, Holwell did not see more permanent development of a keep or walls in stone.

D06 *The well-preserved earthworks of a Norman motte-and-bailey castle at Holwell Castle, Parracombe.*

D07 and D08 **Parracombe Common and Ilkerton Ridge**

East from Parracombe the former commons at Parracombe Common and South Common are amongst many on Exmoor that had their common rights removed through Act of Parliament so that the land could be improved for agriculture. "Common" land was under the control of the lord of the manor, but a number of rights on the land, such as for livestock grazing were variously held by certain nearby properties, or (occasionally) held in gross by all manorial tenants. The majority of the 'Inclosure Acts' were passed in the eighteenth and nineteenth centuries. Compensation meant that rights' holders in many cases supported enclosure, although the poorer people with common rights often received very little or no recompense. Generally, enclosed land is divided into relatively large, rectilinear fields compared to the smaller, more irregular fields of earlier times.

D07 *Field pattern to the east of Parracombe with large, rectilinear fields on the former Parracombe Common.*

D08 *Looking north from Butter Hill. Though not a common, this area is now open moorland although the name is suggestive of the richness of grazing there in the past.*

D09 **Furzehill**

North and South Furzehill and Furzehill Common lie to the east of Ilkerton Ridge. Furze is an alternative name for gorse.

D09 *Below Roborough, the land descends to the Hoaroak Water valley. Hoaroak Water is a tributary of the East Lyn that joins Farley Water at Hillsford Bridge before joining the East Lyn itself at Watersmeet. Crossing Hoaroak Water at this point is via some tricky stepping stones!*

D09 *Waterwheel at a former mill in North Furzehill fed by Warcombe Water, a tributary of the West Lyn River.*

D09 *Valley of Hoaroak Water in spring.*

D10 and D11 **Cheriton Ridge and Brendon Common**

Taken together, Cheriton Ridge and Brendon Common form the largest area of common land on Exmoor that still has common rights – see page 33.

D10 *A Bronze Age ring cairn with inner kerbing lies near the centre of a saddle on Cheriton Ridge. It is compact and well preserved, 15.8 metres in diameter and 0.5 metres high, though the interior has been disturbed[1].*

D10 *Farley Water separates Cheriton Ridge on the left (west) from Brendon Common on the right (east).*

[Facing page] **D12** *Contorted oaks in Badgworthy Wood.*

D12 Badgworthy

The deserted medieval settlement at Badgworthy (pronounced Badgery) is one of the best preserved medieval villages in England. It is thought to be the inspiration for the homestead of the Doone clan in the R.D. Blackmore novel of 1869 (see **C12**).

D12 *Youngsters on the Duke of Edinburgh scheme walking through Badgworthy.*

D12 *Around 14 building platforms from the medieval village of Badgworthy can be seen amongst the bracken. One house was inhabited until 1814.*

D12 *Badgworthy Cottage was built in the 1860s by Frederic Knight as a shepherd's dwelling mainly using stone from the medieval village nearby. The Cottage was occupied until the 1930s. It fell within the area of the Exmoor Firing Ranges during the Second World War and was demolished by heavy artillery shells during practice firing by the United States army.*

D13 and D14 **Stowey Allotment and Mill Hill**

Many areas of Exmoor are known as 'Allotment', the term given to allocations of land following enclosure of a common through an Act of Parliament. Stowey Allotment took on a particular significance in the 1970s when it became the focus of a controversy concerning the ploughing of moorland on Exmoor for agriculture.

It was estimated that some 15% of moorland was lost in the nine years between 1957 and 1966, mostly through agricultural improvement. Towards the end of the 1960s, ploughing of moorland on Exmoor received national attention and it became a conflict between agricultural improvement and conservation of landscape and wildlife. A voluntary agreement was entered into to encourage any farmer intending to reclaim moorland, to notify the National Park Committee six months beforehand to allow time for a negotiation to proceed. Towards the end of 1976 the new owner announced their wish to plough the moorland at Stowey Allotment. The failure in 1977 to come to an agreement to prevent ploughing was followed by a Public Inquiry led by Lord Porchester (see **J14**).

Legislation and government funding for Moorland Management Agreements followed. These agreements, together with purchase of some key moorland areas by the National Park Committee and subsequent designation of much of the remaining moorland areas as Sites of Special Scientific Interest (SSSI), have resulted in a cessation of moorland reclamation within the National Park.[5]

D13 *Chalk Water valley.*

D13 *Boundary between Turf Allotment and Stowey Allotment on the right, showing the impacts of moorland reclamation in the late 1970s.*

D16 *The valley above Pool Bridge. The valley carries water from Nutscale Reservoir* **(E16)** *to Horner Water.*

D15 and D16 Hawkcombe and Pool Bridge

East of Porlock Allotment and south of Porlock Common is the catchment for the Hawkcombe Stream that descends through moor and woods to Porlock. Hawkcombe Head is especially significant for the extensive remains left by Mesolithic (Middle Stone Age) hunter gatherers who used the area for at least 1000 years around 7000 to 8000 years ago. A series of archaeological excavations in the area have recovered very large quantities of late Mesolithic flint, and the evidence for hearths, postholes and stake-holes. Flint does not occur naturally on Exmoor so it is clear that people were bringing the stone to the area to be worked into a variety of stone tools. Other Mesolithic sites have been discovered on Selworthy, Bossington and Porlock Beach and, more recently, at Larkbarrow and Brendon Common, indicating that people at that time ranged widely across what is now Exmoor.[1]

D15 *Archaeological dig in 2013 at Hawkcombe Head, the site of extensive Mesolithic remains.*

D15 *Exmoor Ponies at Hawkcombe Head.*

D16 *Hawkcombe Woods is a National Nature Reserve owing to its importance for wildlife. Recent management of the woodland has improved wildlife habitat by the creation of clearings and retention of deadwood, important for insects and fungi.*

D17 **Horner Woods**

The ancient woodlands at Horner fill the valley either side of Horner Water – a name possibly derived from the Celtic hwrnwr, meaning snorer from the sound of the water in floods. Horner Woods is an ancient woodland and is designated as a National Nature Reserve.

Horner Woods is important for wildlife with a rich variety of invertebrates and birds, such as the Wood Warbler, that favour ancient woodlands.

The large beetle, Stenocorus meridianus, feeds as a larva on diseased wood.

D17 *Paths through Horner Woods in snow.*

Water Crickets, Velia caprai, are small bugs that live on the surface of still waters and puddles and feed on insects that become trapped on the water surface.

D17 *Late medieval packhorse bridge at Horner.*

Common Darter dragonfly.

Caddis fly.

D18 Luccombe

The Domesday Book records that the manor of Locumba (Luccombe) was held by Queen Edith at the time of King Edward and it was then held by Ralph de Limesi, one of the companions of William the Conqueror at the Norman invasion.[1] Today, it falls within the Holnicote estate owned by The National Trust.

In 1944, Luccombe was the subject of a study undertaken by 'Mass Observation', a social research organisation founded in 1937. The study recorded the accounts of Luccombe residents about their lives and was covered in a book entitled *Exmoor Village* in 1947.[6]

D18 *Village of Luccombe. St Mary's church has a thirteenth century chancel.*

D19 *Tivington lies to the east of Porlock Vale where much of the farmland is suitable for arable crops.*

D19 **Blackford and Tivington**

D19
Combine harvester in the fields at Blackford.

D19 *[Above, right] St Leonard's Chapel, Tivington, is in the manor of Blackford, and some two miles from the parish church at Selworthy. It was probably built about 1340-1360 by Sir Ralph de Midelney as a 'Chapel-of-Ease' for use by people who could not reach the parish church easily. The chapel was secularised after the Reformation in the sixteenth century, when a fireplace was inserted and an extension built on the east end. The chapel was restored in 1896 and reconsecrated in 1940.*

D19 *[Right] The dovecote at Blackford was probably built in the fifteenth century. With 302 nest boxes, the dovecote would have provided an important source of eggs and meat (the young pigeons or 'squabs' were eaten), and droppings for fertiliser. Blackford mansion house burnt down in 1875 and the site is now occupied by modern farm buildings.*

D20 to D21 **Periton Hill and Alcombe Common**

Much of the high ground that lies between Tivington and Dunster is now dominated by conifer plantations apart from the highest ridge that remains as open heathland.

D20 *Periton Hill in snow.*

D21 *Alcombe Common.*

D21 *Red deer stag on Alcombe Common during the rut in October. Minehead lies in the background.*

D22 Conygar Hill, Dunster

D22 *Conygar Tower was built around 1775. It was designed by Richard Phelps to enhance the landscape around Dunster Castle, which was then owned by H. F. Luttrell. It cost £76 11s 1/2d to build; £4 2s 6d in scrumpy (cider) for the workmen, and an entertainment when it was complete cost £2 5s.[1]*

Conygar Hill lies immediately to the north of Dunster. Coney is the Middle English name for rabbit and the name of the hill suggests that it had been used as a rabbit warren. The Normans are thought to have introduced rabbits for food and raised the animals in warrens which were known as coneygarths. The term 'rabbit', derived from medieval French *rabette*, was used until the eighteenth century only to refer to juveniles, which were a culinary delicacy.[7]

D22 *Conygar Tower from below.*

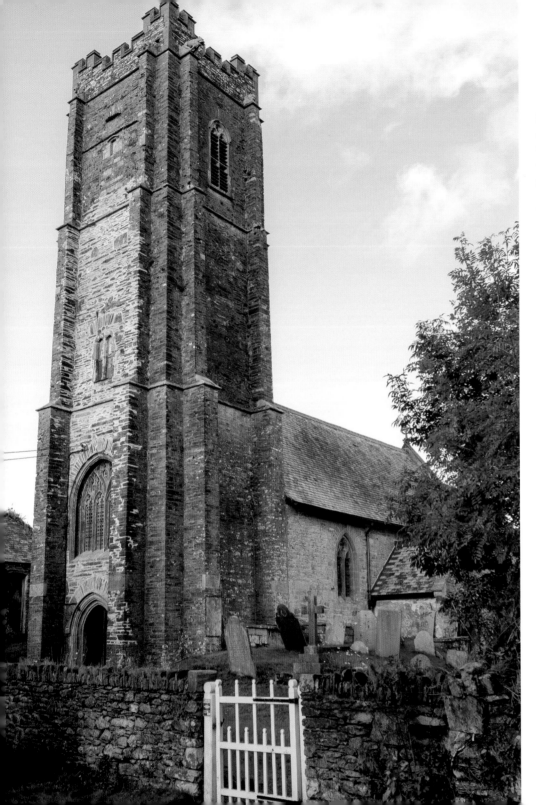

E04 Kentisbury

Kentisbury lies on the western boundary of the National Park. The impressive west tower of St Thomas's church dates from the late 1400s or early 1500s as does the nave and south porch.

E04 *Kentisbury church pulpit.*

E04 *Triptych above the altar at Kentisbury church.*

E04 *Tall tower of Kentisbury church.*

E05 and E06 **Blackmoor Gate**

Blackmoor is the modern spelling, the area having been named Blackmore in previous centuries as it was part of the Blackmore estate. The name was changed when, in 1895, Henry Blackmore unsuccessfully petitioned against the Act of Parliament for the building of the Lynton and Barnstaple Railway through his estate. Following his objection, the railway station eventually built here was named 'Blackmoor' Gate.[1] The former station is now the Old Station Inn although there are plans to restore the railway and return the inn to a station once more.

Since 1989, there has been an open-air livestock market at Blackmoor Gate operated by the Exmoor Farmers Livestock Auctions Ltd (see page 106). The busiest time of year is the autumn sheep sales.

E06 *The Holwell valley south of Parracombe. The Bronze Age Holwell Barrow can be made out on the horizon on the former Challacombe North Common which was finally enclosed in 1859 after an initial phase in 1791.[8] As with many other parts of Exmoor, the former commons east of Kentisbury and south of Parracombe were gradually enclosed during the 1700s and 1800s.*

E05 *A wet autumn day at Blackmoor Gate market sheep sales.*

E07 and E08 **Chapman Barrows and the Long Stone**

The high ground to the east of Challacombe Common provides some of the most striking archaeology on Exmoor with a series of Bronze Age monuments including 12 barrows forming a linear cemetery; a setting of five stones known as the quincunx; the 3-metre-high Long Stone, and the large Longstone Barrow.

E07 *The quincunx is made up of five standing stones arranged in a pattern that resembles the spots on the five face on a playing dice. Unfortunately, the stones are difficult to find and appear to have been damaged in recent years.*

E07 *Barrow 9 in the Bronze Age Chapman Barrows complex with Ordnance Survey Trig Point.*

[Facing page] **E08** *The Long Stone is propped by a substantial trigger stone at the base. The stone's relationship to the surrounding barrows and landscape is likely to have been highly significant to the people who erected the stone – the largest standing stone in the area.*

E09 Pinkery Pond

Pinkery Pond was constructed by placing an earth dam across the headwaters of the River Barle sometime after John Knight had purchased the Exmoor Forest from the Crown in 1818-20. The original purpose for the construction is not certain, although it is presumed to be linked to the construction of the 'Prayway canal', which starts near Pinkery Pond. The Prayway canal was partially constructed in winter 1819/20 along with the Warren canal, as part of major early works that followed John Knight's acquisition of the Royal Forest (see page 98). The two canals were probably intended to transport materials, such as lime, needed in the improvement of the surrounding land for agriculture. Ultimately, however, while substantial sections were excavated, the canal system was not completed and never came into use.

The pond has been emptied twice by removing the plugs that block two drainage pipes within a 170m tunnel installed as part of the dam construction. On the first occasion, in 1889, the body of a Parracombe farmer, Richard Gammin, was recovered. On the second occasion, in 1913, the pond was drained in the course of a search for a suspected suicide of a man from Exford. In this case, no body was found in the pond and it was six months before the body of the missing man was discovered in a mine adit.[1]

Pinkery Pond drains into the River Barle, a tributary of the Exe that flows south to Exmouth on the English Channel coast a distance of around 96 kilometres (60 miles).

E09 *West Lyn River at Ruckham Combe. A little to the north of Pinkery Pond, Ruckham Combe drains into the West Lyn River that flows northwards just 8 kilometres (5 miles) to the Bristol Channel at Lynmouth.*

E09 *The dam at Pinkery Pond. Water levels in the pond are significantly lower than the top of the dam as the pond now drains through a channel cut through the rock that can be seen on the left in the picture.*

E10 Hoar Oak

The original Hoar Oak tree was probably one of a number marking the boundary of the former Royal Forest and the commons of Lynton and Brendon. An oak tree still stands close to the site of the original but is presumed to have been planted around 100 years or so ago. 'Hoar' is probably derived from 'ore' meaning a boundary, for the Hoar Oak tree marks not only the boundary of the Royal Forest and commons to the north, but also the boundary between Somerset and Devon counties and between Lynton and Brendon parishes.[9]

Hoar Oak Water flows northwards past the oak on its way to join the East Lyn River at Watersmeet. A short distance north of the tree are the remains of a farmhouse that was probably constructed sometime in the early nineteenth century. According to the Tithe Apportionment for Lynton of 1839, the house and land around it was owned by John Vellacott. The farm was leased to Frederic Knight sometime after 1867, who installed a Scottish Shepherd here and used it as a base for his sheep flock on The Chains. It was the longest-lived of the Knight family's herdings and the house was not abandoned until 1959. Having fallen into ruin, the house remains were stabilised in 2013/14 to provide a memorial to the people who lived and worked in this remote location.[10]

E10 *Hoar Oak Cottage after consolidation work in 2013/14.*

Hoaroak Water arises in Long Chains Combe which has some intriguing ruins on a promontory at its eastern end. Labelled 'sheepfold' on the Ordnance Survey map, a recent survey of the structure interprets it as the lost Hoar Oak Cottage in Exmoor parish (different to the Hoar Oak Cottage to the north in the parish of Lynton and Lynmouth). The dimensions and layout are very similar to other agricultural workers' cottages built on Exmoor by John Knight in the 1820s and 1830s. It is recorded in the 1841 census returns as housing four Irish labourers, but is not mentioned on any other census returns. The labourers were employed to work at the nearby 'gate-post factory' where stone outcrops were quarried for use on the Exmoor Forest estate.

E10 *Hoar Oak Water below the Hoar Oak tree.*

E10 *The small promontory at the foot of Long Chains Combe showing the ruins of a cottage (not sheepfold) on the summit.*

E11 Brendon Two Gates and Mire Restoration Project

E11 *Brendon Two Gates.*

Brendon Two Gates marks the boundary between Somerset and Devon.

During the Second World War an area of over 22 square kilometres was used for military training including Brendon Common, Malmsmead Hill, Hoccombe Hill, Badgworthy Hill, Lanacombe, Trout Hill and as far east as Toms Hill and Larkbarrow. Ranges were initially used by the British and later by United States artillery. Between May 1941 and June 1943, British chemical warfare groups used the ranges and were engaged in developing projectiles for the delivery of chemical warheads by improving on the 'Livens Projector' which had been developed in the First World War. Test firings included 'Livens' projectiles (see page 70), but the 5-inch rocket was developed as a more effective method for mass deployment of chemical weapons. The remains of 5-inch rockets are still found regularly on the former ranges.

A short way to the north of Brendon Two Gates is a granite memorial to Colonel MacLaren of the Royal Engineers. Colonel MacLaren threw himself onto an explosive device that went wrong when it was being demonstrated to Government officials and fellow officers. He was killed instantly, but no one else was hurt. A memorial stone was erected on the spot, with an inscription reading: *"In memory of Colonel R.H. Maclaren, O.B.E. M.C. Commander C.W. Troops Royal Engineers, who was killed on duty on this spot May 20 1941. This stone was erected by his brother officers."*[1]

E11 *Remains of a Second World War 5-inch rocket on Brendon Common.*

E11 *The MacLaren memorial on Brendon Common.*

Brendon Common is one of the best locations on Exmoor for observing dark skies on a clear night – see pages 66 and 67.

E11 Mire Restoration Project

Over the last 3000-5000 years, the central moorlands of Exmoor have accumulated a blanket of peat which is over a metre deep in places. Peat is formed when plant remains build up in wet, nutrient-poor mire habitats such as blanket bogs, valley bogs and fens. The most common mire type on Exmoor is blanket bog, with over 30 km² present.[11]

Historically, the blanket bogs have been drained to provide better access for grazing livestock and areas where peat can be cut and dried to provide fuel for domestic fires. At Blackpits, there are extensive remains of former peat cutting areas with characteristic straight-sided depressions up to a metre deep. Over time, however, the improved drainage exposes the peat to air and leads to drying out and oxidation so that the stored carbon is released into the atmosphere.

Since the 1990s, a series of projects have sought to block up drainage ditches on moorland areas to re-wet the peat and stimulate the growth of the bog grasses and sphagnum moss once again. The anticipated benefits to this work include: more water storage; improved water quality; carbon storage in the peat, and improved habitats for wetland wildlife.

E11 *Square depression resulting from past peat digging for domestic fuel.*

E11 *Small pools, sphagnum moss and cotton grass resulting from raised water levels across the peatland areas at Blackpits.*

The Black Darter is Britain's smallest dragonfly and is restricted to acidic shallow pools such as those found on moorland blanket bog. The rewetting of the peat has increased the habitat for this species on Exmoor. The males are almost wholly black while the females and immatures are mainly yellow in colour.

Exmoor's Dark Skies

Exmoor is one of the most sparsely populated areas in southern England. The relatively low level of built development means that there is little light pollution and excellent views of the night sky on clear nights.

Following a thorough assessment by the International Dark Sky Association, the heart of the National Park was designated Europe's first International Dark Sky Reserve in Autumn 2011.

The full moon rising over Dunkery Beacon. The series of pictures was taken on 14 May having selected a time and position where it was expected that the moon would rise behind the Beacon. Moonrise was expected at 20.41 but the height of the hill meant that it was around 30 minutes later when the moon could first be seen. Once visible, it took only five minutes or so for the moon to rise clear of the horizon.

Facing page: An image of the Milky Way taken from Valley of Rocks, Lynton. The bright spot just above the horizon left of centre is the planet Mars.

E12 Lanacombe and Trout Hill

Lanacombe and Trout Hill lie within the former Exmoor Forest and were subject to considerable efforts at agricultural improvement during the middle of the nineteenth century, including many miles of small drainage ditches (for more on the Exmoor Forest see pages 98-99). The harsh winters and high rainfall mean that the vegetation cover has since become dominated by the coarse purple moorgrass (Molinia), known locally as the 'grassmoor'.

Buscombe Beeches is an unusual feature on the south facing slopes of Lanacombe. It is made up of four stone-lined earth banks and measures around 100 by 75 metres. The four sides all curve inwards and the corners are projected and topped by beech hedges. It is thought to be a sheep enclosure, although very different from the smaller circular structures more usual across Exmoor. Similar structures to Buscombe Beeches are located in the Borders of Scotland, suggesting that this sheepfold was created by the Scottish shepherds who were brought to Exmoor by Frederic Knight sometime during the 1860.[1 and 8]

E12 *Confluence of Badgworthy Water and Hoccombe Water below Trout Hill.*

Lanacombe and Trout Hill contain a range of archaeological sites including stone settings, enclosures and cairns. An excavation in 2009 found a small cist (burial chamber) within one of the stone cairns. Some charcoal remains found inside the cist gave radiocarbon dates of 2460-2190 BC indicating that the cairn was built in the late Neolithic.

E12 *Buscombe Beeches, an unusual, four-sided sheepfold on Lanacombe.*

E12 *Remains of the cist found within a Neolithic cairn on Lanacombe in 2009.*

E13 and E14 **Great Tom's Hill and Kittuck Meads**

E14 *Panorama taken from inside the Kittuck Meads sheepfold. Kittuck Meads sheepfold is also circular but has a beech hedge on its bank that is now overgrown. The structure is documented as having been constructed shortly after 1878 when a lot of sheep were lost in severe snowstorms[1].*

Moving eastwards from Trout Hill, the moor continues over Great Tom's Hill towards Larkbarrow. Despite modern disturbance, including use of the area for military training in Second World War, a range of archaeological features can be seen across the area. These include the mysterious 'stone settings' which appear to be unique to Exmoor. The settings are small groups of relatively small upright stones that it is thought date back to the Neolithic around 4000 years ago.

As well as their origins, the purpose of the settings is also a mystery.

E13 *Pinford, a nineteenth-century feature that encircles a natural outcrop of the bedrock. Circular sheepfolds are more typical than the much larger structure at Buscombe Beeches on the previous page.*

E13 *Stone setting on Great Tom's Hill. The setting has at least six standing stones, four of which can be seen in the photograph. Manor Allotment is in the background.*

E14 *Stone rubble – all that remains of Larkbarrow Farm surrounded by beech trees.*

E14 *A section of the 'V' shaped trench on Porlock Allotment constructed during use of the area for military training in the Second World War.*

When John Knight completed the purchase of Exmoor Forest from the Crown in 1820, he set about the large-scale improvement of the land for agriculture (see page 98). In the 1840s, John Knight's son Frederic Knight changed the approach to one where a large part of the estate was divided into a series of farmsteads to be let under 'improving tenancies' where tenants would receive some compensation for work they undertook to further improve the land. Larkbarrow was let on Lady's Day 1849 to James Meadows who came from Leicestershire. He succeeded in producing wheat and stilton cheese but had to leave in 1852 when his dairy business failed. The farm was not re-let and remained uninhabited until the 1860s when shepherds brought from Scotland lived on the farm, which then operated as one of several 'herdings' on the estate.

The farmhouse was commissioned for military training in Second World War and was used for target practice by artillery. The ruins were later demolished and all that remains of Larkbarrow Farm are a few lengths of standing wall and the footings of former outbuildings plus the beech trees planted for shelter. The surrounding fields have not been much changed since the war, making the field system at Larkbarrow the most complete of Frederic Knight's farms to survive.

Porlock Allotment to the east of Larkbarrow also formed part of the military training area. Remains from this time include a 'V' shaped trench with two arms around 250 metres long and 2 metres across. The exact function is not known but it might have been used for moving targets for artillery training.[1]

[Facing page] **E14** *Beech trees marking the ruins of Larkbarrow seen from Porlock Allotment.*

Exmoor's Red Deer

Stag with hinds during the autumn rut.

The red deer is the largest native wild land animal in Britain and would have been an important prey item for the Mesolithic people who inhabited Exmoor around 8000 years ago. It is likely that Saxon nobles would have hunted deer on Exmoor well before the more formal establishment of a Royal Forest after the Norman Conquest.

The Forest laws imposed by the Normans sought to preserve the 'vert' (woodland vegetation) and 'venison' (principle game species) for the benefit of the Crown. On Exmoor, Forest laws were administered through the Swaincote Court which met alternately near Landacre Bridge and in Hawkridge churchyard and dealt with minor charges. More serious offences were tried at the Forest Eyre usually held in Ilchester every three years. At the Eyre in 1270, 64 offenders were charged with *'destruction of the Vert of Exmore'* and most received fines. There were 15 cases involving the deer of Exmoor and Hugh of Luccombe was declared to be *'an evil doer to the venison of the Lord King'* and detained in prison. There are no records of any king hunting on Exmoor in person, although in 1315 Edward II sent an order to the sheriff of Somerset to provide *'of Exmore 20 stags'*.[13]

In 1508, Henry VII leased the Forest to Sir Edmund Carew, a Devon knight, allowing him to hunt deer so long as at least 100 were maintained. Hunting and enforcement of forest law was then managed locally by Wardens of the forest until the Forest's enclosure and sale in 1818.[13]

Improvement of the former Royal Forest for agriculture after 1818, and enclosure of some of the surrounding commons, led to a decline in red deer and numbers in central Exmoor fell below 100. The recovery of the deer commenced after 1855 when landowners came together to form the Devon & Somerset Staghounds and stag hunting became a major social and recreational activity. By 1900 red deer numbers were estimated at around 1500. Deer numbers declined during the Second World War when much of Exmoor's moorland was taken over for military training but increased again after the war with the cooperation of the farming community when hunting resumed.

The best time to view red deer is during the autumn breeding season known as the 'rut' that starts towards the end of September through to November. At this time, individual stags take up small territories and attract a group of hinds (female red deer).

Occasional fights can happen between evenly-matched stags for possession of the territory but, more often, the larger stag will be able to ward off a smaller rival in a display of 'parallel-walking' that enables each stag to size up the other.

As well as larger size, the antlers gain more branches known as 'points'. A good antler will have a strong shaft with a 'brow'

Larger stag with a group of hinds 'parallel walking' with a younger stag that has strayed too close. In cases like this, where the size disparity between stags is so great, the smaller stag usually departs to a safe distance without a fight.

Some impressive stags in August with their antlers still covered in velvet.

point branching near the head, a 'bey' point in the middle and a 'trey' above. Above that, the antler of a mature stag branches into a series of further points so that each antler of a 'Royal' stag has a brow, bey and trey with three points above – referred to as "All his rights and three atop" on Exmoor.

A mature Exmoor stag with particularly large antlers showing the brow, bey and trey points along the length of the antler and five points at the top – "All his rights and five atop".

Hinds and calves on Dunkery in November.

Hinds give birth in late May to July. Each hind finds a secure place of cover to give birth to her single calf (twins are very rare). The calf spends the first week or so concealed in vegetation with the hind visiting every few hours to suckle. After about ten days, the calf is strong enough to follow the hind and, by late summer and autumn, the hinds and calves often come together in small herds.

After the rut, the hinds and stags tend to group together in single-sex herds. The stags' antlers fall off in late March and April. As soon as the old antlers are shed a new set begins to grow. As they grow, the antlers are covered in a thick skin called 'velvet' that contains blood vessels and nerves to supply the rapidly growing bone. By August the new growth will be complete and the antler hardens into solid bone and the velvet is shed. A large pair of antlers can weigh up to 9 kilograms – grown in just four months.

In recent years, annual counts of the red deer across Exmoor have totalled around 3000. The number of deer and the tolerance of damage and loss of farm crops that they cause, reflects the continuing importance of red deer and hunting to Exmoor's local culture. Many local pubs, hotels, homes and public buildings display stag trophies; the stag's head was the chosen logo for the National Park, and stags are frequently included in local artworks. A competition for the best sets of found antlers is held annually at Exford Show (see page 116).

Gate ornament in Dunster.

Weathervane in Brendon.

[Facing page] **E15**
Ice covered hedgerow near Lucott Cross after freezing rain.

E15 *View towards Dunkery Hill from Alderman's Barrow Allotment.*

Alderman's Barrow Allotment and the moorland beyond provides the catchment for Nutscale Reservoir. The reservoir was built in 1942 to help relieve summer droughts in Minehead and supply Porlock and Minehead.

Stoke Pero is referred to in the Domesday Book as Stoche. Pero was added after Gilbert Pero, resident in 1280. The list of rectors goes back to 1242 and the existing tower dates from the thirteenth century, although the remainder of the church was largely rebuilt in 1897 and restored again in 1955. When the new foundations were dug in 1897, three sets of human remains were uncovered from directly under the old north wall, suggesting that the thirteenth century church had been built on the site of an older churchyard.[1]

E16 *Stoke Pero church is the highest on Exmoor at 307 metres (1013 feet). It has been claimed to be the highest in England but that is incorrect as the church in Flash, Staffordshire, is substantially higher at 460 metres abive sea level.*

E16 *Nutscale Reservoir receives its water from a series of secluded combes.*

E17 and E18 **Dunkery Hill's Northern Slopes**

E18 *Large Bronze Age cairn known as Robin How on Luccombe Hill with Joaney How in the background.*

[Left} **E17** *Looking south to Dunkery Beacon from above Horner Woods.*

The northern slopes of Dunkery descending to the Horner valley which is heavily wooded and designated as a National Nature Reserve.

The area above Horner is rich with remains of prehistoric and medieval settlements such as those at Bagley and Sweetworthy. Further east, Luccombe Hill has many burial cairns dated to the

E18 *Remains of a cairn on Luccombe Hill looking towards Wootton Courtenay.*

Bronze Age. Two of the largest cairns are named Robin How and Joaney How, possibly a reference to Robin Hood and Little John.

E19 *Panorama of Wootton Courtenay with the ridge behind formed by Periton, Knowle and Grabbist hills. The prominent circle on the slopes above the village was formed by a commemorative ring of beech trees*

Wootton Courtenay was known as Otone in the Domesday Book meaning settlement by the wood. Courtenay was added in the about 1280 when Hugh de Courtenay held the manor.[4]

The village lies to the south of a high ridge formed by Periton Hill, Knowle Hill and Grabbist Hill. The majority of the ridge is planted with conifers with the remains of the former heathland on the ridge summit.

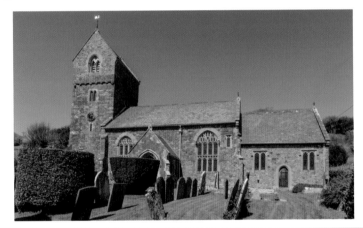

[Right] **E19** *Wootton Courtenay church dates from the thirteenth century with a nave added in the fifteenth century though it was much altered in the mid-1800s. The gabled tower is an unusual feature shared by Stoke Pero* **(E16)** *and Churchtown, Luxborough* **(H21)** *churches on Exmoor.*

E20 and E21 **Timberscombe**

Timberscombe means 'wooded valley' and is noted in the Domesday Book as Timbrescumbe.

A watermill has been in existence at Cowbridge at least since the early fourteenth century, when it was named in a deed concerning some land belonging to Dunster Priory. It was recorded as a flour mill as part of the Knowle estate in 1567. In 1904, part of the mill was converted into a house (Hill View). A garage was built at the site in the 1920s and the water wheel supplied electricity until the late 1930s.[1] Recently, the waterwheel has been brought back into operation and a range of water-powered machinery installed.

E20 *Some of the water powered machinery at Cowbridge Mill, Timberscombe.*

E20 *Timberscombe church is predominantly fifteenth century. It is dedicated to St Petrock as is the church at Churchtown, Parracombe (D06).*

E20 *The rich fan-vaulted screen at Timberscombe is one of a group made about 1500, probably at Dunster, of which seven still exist.*

E21 *View north over Minehead from the ridge above Alcombe Common.*

The name Dunster derives from an earlier name Torre ("tor, rocky hill"). The origin of the prefix is uncertain, although it may well refer to 'Dunn', a Saxon noble who held land nearby before the Norman conquest, giving 'Dunestore' meaning 'Dunn's craggy hill'.[1]

To the south of the village are several Iron Age hillforts showing evidence of early human occupation. These include Bat's Castle and Black Ball Camp on Gallox Hill.[1]

Dunster grew up around the castle which was built on the Tor by the Norman warrior William de Mohun shortly after the Norman Conquest of 1066. He constructed a motte-and-bailey castle similar to the one that can still be seen in Parracombe **(D06)** with timber defences. A stone keep was built on the motte by the early 1100s.

At the end of the fourteenth century the de Mohuns sold the castle to the Luttrell family, who continued to occupy the property until the late twentieth century. During the English Civil War, Dunster was initially held as a garrison for the Royalists. It fell to the Parliamentarians in 1645 and orders were sent out for the castle to be demolished. However, these were not carried out, and the castle remained the garrison for Parliamentarian troops until 1650. The present castle buildings were thoroughly reconstructed from around 1617 onwards with major alterations in 1747 and extensive enlargement and remodelling in 1869-72.

E22 *The gatehouse to Dunster castle was built in 1420 by Sir Hugh Luttrell and is one of the older parts of the castle.*

E22 *View of Dunster from Bat's Castle looking towards the Bristol Channel and South Wales. Dunster Castle is to the right, Priory church left of centre and Conygar Tower in the centre.*

E22 Dunster

As well as founding the castle, William de Mohun built the first church in Dunster and gave the church and the tithes of several manors and two fisheries to the Benedictine Abbey at Bath. Dunster Priory, situated just north of the church, became a cell of the abbey. The Priory church of St George, dovecote and tithe barn are all relics from the Priory. In 1332 it became more separated from the Abbey at Bath and became a priory in its own right.

E22 The dovecote was probably built in the late sixteenth century.

Dunster had become an important centre for wool cloth production by the thirteenth century, with the market dating back to at least 1222. A particular kind of kersey or broadcloth became known as 'Dunsters'. The Yarn Market was probably built in 1609 to maintain the importance of the village as a market.

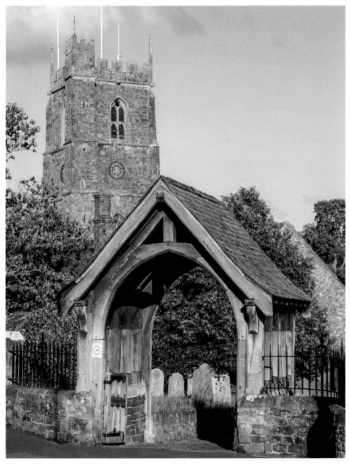

E22 The Priory church of St George is predominantly fifteenth century with evidence of twelfth and thirteenth century work.

E22 The Yarn Market is an octagonal building constructed around a central pier. The building contains a hole in one of the roof beams, the result of cannon fire in the Civil War. A bell at the top was rung to indicate the start of trading.

Dunster Show

The Dunster Show was founded in 1835 and takes place annually on the third Friday in August at Dunster Castle Lawns. Local breeds of sheep and cattle are a major feature of the show.

Starting young – a young contestant receiving a rosette at the 2016 show.

Looking across the sheep pens towards Dunster Castle.

The Exmoor Horn sheep is the hardy native sheep of Exmoor that was developed in the nineteenth century. As well as being reared for meat, the Exmoor Horn produces a fine quality wool fleece. Many Exmoor farms mate the Exmoor Horn ewe with a Blue-faced Leicester ram to produce crossbreed lambs known as 'mules'.

The Red Devon or Red Ruby is the distinctive traditional breed of cattle for North Devon. A mature bull can weigh between 700 and 1000 kilograms. The Red Devon is a hardy animal that can thrive on relatively poor fodder making them ideal for rougher pastures.

Exmoor Horn ram and Class 161 winner in 2014 looking very pleased with himself!

A Red Devon bull in the show ring.

F06 and F07 **Challacombe**

Challacombe parish lies on the western boundary of the National Park. The name appears in the Domesday Book as Celdecombe meaning Cold Valley from the Olde English ceald for cold.

Holy Trinity church, Challa-combe, occupies an isolated position adjacent to Barton Town farmhouse some 1.2 kilometres to the east of the main village of Challacombe. Historical evidence suggests that this wasn't the case when the church was first founded when there were small settlements nearby.

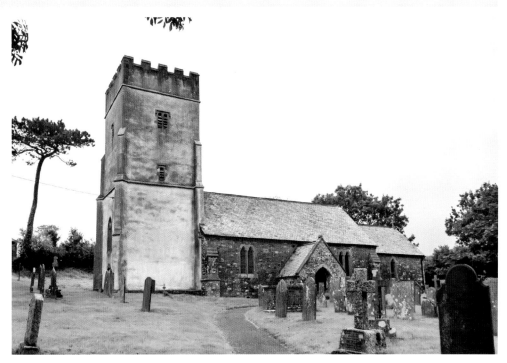

F06 *Challacombe church was largely rebuilt in 1850, and was subsequently restored in 1874-5. Only the west tower remains of the earlier church.*

F07 *The 'Black Venus' in Challacombe.*

F07 *Challacombe Methodist chapel was built in 1868 as a Bible Christian Chapel. The Bible Christians were founded in the early 1800s in North Cornwall and Devon as an independent branch of the Methodists. In 1932, the Methodists were united and the chapel changed its affiliation.*

F09 *To the north east of Pinkery lies Chains Barrow, a prominent Bronze Age bowl barrow being a central mound surrounded by a ditch.*

F08 and F09 Edgerley Stone and Chains Barrow

Just over 4 kilometres west of Challacombe, a large rough stone about 5 feet high stands in the northern bank of the road from Challacombe to Simonsbath (B3358). Until the enclosure of the Forest in 1819 or of Challacombe Common in 1857, it had stood alone on the open moor, probably since Saxon times. This boundary stone is called 'Longstone' in 1651 in a Survey of Exmoor Chase, but is given the name 'Edgerley Stone' on the 1675 Map of Exmoor. The stone defines many boundaries, including the Challacombe and High Bray Commons, the Exmoor-Challacombe parish boundary and the western boundary of the Forest of Exmoor, as well as the Somerset-Devon county boundary[1].

F09 *Pinkery Farm was the most westerly dwelling in Somerset when it was built in around 1850 as part of the development of the former Royal Forest by Frederic Knight (see G11). The former farm is now an outdoor centre operated by Exmoor National Park Authority.*

F08 *The Edgerley Stone set into the road bank. The only inscriptions on the stone appear to be F. BRAY and F. ISAAC, which were probably the names of the men employed in making the modern fences.*

F10 Exe Head and Tangs Bottom

The high ridge of The Chains extends eastward from Chains Barrow and forms the watershed between streams and rivers draining to the Bristol Channel in the north and the River Barle and Exe that drain south to the English Channel. Even today, this area can seem wild and remote. Many of us regard these qualities positively but it wasn't always the case. In his tour of England, Daniel Defoe writes, "*Leaving the coast, we came, in our going southward, to the great river Ex, or Isca, which rises in this north side of the country, and that so far as, like the Tamar, it begins within four or five miles of the Severn Sea: the country it rises in, is called Exmore, Cambden calls it a filthy, barren, ground, and, indeed, so it is...*"

F10 *The source of the River Exe at Exe Head is a spring emerging from a small mire west of Dure Down. A stone has been installed recently to mark the spot. From here, the stream starts its journey of over 95 kilometres (60 miles) to eventually reach the English Channel at Exmouth.*

F10 *Just south of Exe Head the small stream in the Tangs Bottom valley is a tributary of the River Barle. The Barle joins the Exe just to the south of the National Park above Exebridge (page 175).*

F11 Prayway Head and Simonsbath Tower

F11 *Despite being a small stream in the present day, the headwaters of the Exe have eroded a sizable valley at Prayway Head. The boundary between the Hangman Sandstone (shallow slopes to the left) and Ilfracombe Slates (steep slopes to the right) runs along the river valley.[3]*

F11 *South from Prayway Head just west of the road to Simonsbath, lies the ' Simonsbath Tower; a small circular structure built during the phase of reclamation of Exmoor Forest by the Knights. The function of the tower is not known.*

F12, F13 and F14 **Upper Exe Valley**

F12 *The Warren at Warren Farm taken from Little Ashcombe.*

F14 *View over Wellshead.*

F13 *A number of Exmoor valleys have interesting geological features where a knoll or ridge of rock stands out from the valley floor. Confusingly, these features are often named 'barrows' even though they are not related to the prehistoric barrows constructed by humans. A good example of a 'geological' barrow is the Long Barrow in the valley of the Exe downstream from Warren Farm.*

F15 and F16 Almsworthy and the Rowbarrows

F15 *Almsworthy Common lies to the south east of Alderman's Barrow. A relatively conspicuous stone setting can be seen on the common, a type of ancient monument unique to Exmoor (see page 69).*

F16 *Around 1.5 kilometres west of Dunkery Beacon there are The Rowbarrows, a set of four Bronze Age burial cairns, sadly much disturbed. The photograph was taken during a November sunrise.*

F17 Dunkery Beacon

Dunkery Beacon is the highest point in Exmoor and Somerset at 519 metres (1703 feet). At the summit of the hill is a large Bronze Age cairn, 34 metres by 27 metres, surmounted by a memorial cairn erected in 1935. In the Middle Ages the hill top was the location for a fire beacon used for signalling.[1]

In February 1917, Sir Charles Thomas Dyke Acland, 12th Baronet, granted a 500-year lease

F17 *Small herd of red deer on Dunkery at sunrise. The young male deer with small antlers are known as prickets.*

of almost 8000 acres of the picturesque Holnicote estate on Exmoor, *"one of the most beautiful pieces of wild country to be found in England"*, to the National Trust, in order to preserve it from future development. The lease was converted into an outright gift thirty-five years later by Sir Richard Thomas Dyke Acland, 15th Baronet (1906-1990), who also donated the estate at Killerton.

Sir Richard was Liberal MP for Barnstaple from 1935 but left the Liberals in 1942 to found the socialist Common Wealth Party along with J.B. Priestley and other political thinkers who were opposed to the wartime coalition of the three main parties. The Common Wealth Party stood on a manifesto of common ownership and morality in politics and had some influence during the war years.

However, only one Common Wealth MP was elected in the General Election of 1945 and many members left the party, including Sir Richard. He joined the Labour Party and won the seat of Gravesend in a by-election in 1947. He held the seat until 1955 when he resigned from Labour because of its support for the then government's nuclear defence policy. Sir Richard subsequently became a founder member of the Campaign for Nuclear Disarmament (CND).

The plaque on the cairn at the summit of Dunkery states, *"Erected in September 1935 to commemorate the handing over to the National Trust for places of historic interest or natural beauty of Dunkery Hill for the benefit of the Nation by Sir Thomas Acland (Baronet), Colonel Wiggin and Allan Hughes Esq."* Lieutenant-Colonel Walter William Wiggin was Master of the Devon & Somerset Staghounds from 1917 to 1936. Allan Hughes was a ship owner and built the country house at West Lynch near Bossington. He was the owner of 1000 acres of moorland included with the Acland land in the gift to the National Trust.

F17 *Memorial cairn at Dunkery Beacon – a popular destination.*

F18 and F19 South East Dunkery

To the south east of Dunkery, the small valleys of Hanny Combe, Spangate, Bin Combe and Mansley Combe drain into the River Aville that flows to the sea north of Dunster. The sheltered combes provide habitat for dragonflies and butterflies, including the rare Heath Fritillary butterfly.

A Golden-ringed dragonfly in Bin Combe

[Below] **F19** *Elsworthy Allotment above Hanny Combe with view north to Wootton Courtenay.*

F18 *Mansley Combe provides the headwaters of the River Aville.*

The Small Fritillary Butterflies

Exmoor is an important stronghold for the Heath Fritillary in Britain.

The Heath Fritillary was once a widespread butterfly but, in the late 1970s, it almost became extinct in Britain. By 1980, only 31 colonies remained, three-quarters of which were fairly small. It is now confined to a few woods in south-east England and some moorland sites on Exmoor and a few other locations in the South-West.[14]

On Exmoor, it is found in sheltered valleys where its foodplant, Common Cow-wheat, grows in vegetation dominated by Bilberry. Half of the colonies on Exmoor were lost between 1989 and 2000 as a reduction in grazing and controlled burning allowed gorse and bracken to overwhelm the cow-wheat and Bilberry. Since then, better management of the habitat has led to some recovery.[14]

Mating Heath Fritillary butterflies showing the underwing pattern.

The other small fritillary butterfly that you are likely to see on Exmoor is the Small-Pearl-bordered Fritillary. While this species has declined by around 60% since 1976, it is still relatively widespread in western Britain. Its preferred habitat is wet areas with its foodplant Marsh Violet. On Exmoor, it can be found in small wet flushes in combes and river valleys.

Unfortunately, the single colony of Marsh Fritillary butterflies present on Exmoor in 2007 seems to have died out. However, it is possible that small numbers might still persist where the habitat conditions are suitable.

The three larger Fritillary butterfly species found on Exmoor are shown on page 12.

Small Pearl-bordered Fritillary butterfly showing upper wing pattern

Small Pearl-bordered Fritillary butterfly underwing.

F20 and F21 Timberscombe Common and Croydon Hill

Even today, roads that cross the high ground of Exmoor are few in number, particularly in the centre of Exmoor. In previous centuries, maintenance of roads was the responsibility of the parish. Improvement of the road infrastructure was very piecemeal and problems became particularly acute on the principal roads between major towns. The remedy that emerged in the late seventeenth century was to establish toll or 'turnpike' roads, where charges on users paid for road construction and maintenance. The bodies charged with managing the turnpike roads were established by separate Acts of Parliament.

The Minehead Turnpike Trust was created in 1765 to maintain main routes in West Somerset and Exmoor. In 1822, an Act of Parliament was passed *"for amending and repairing the Roads from Minehead in the County of Somerset, to Batham Bridge in the Town of Bampton in the County of Devon; and for making a new Branch of Road to communicate therewith."*.[15] The new branch of road is now the A396 from Dunster to Exebridge. Milestones and toll houses were installed along the roads and some can still be seen including the milestone just south of Timberscombe and the toll house at Chilly Bridge south of Bridgetown **(K19)**.

F20 *View north from Oaktrow towards Periton Hill.*

F21 *An area of harvested conifers on Croydon Hill.*

F20 *Milestone on the A396 south of Timberscombe installed by the Minehead Turnpike Trust following the construction of the new road from Dunster to Hele Bridge in the 1820s. Around 9 of the original Minehead Turnpike Trust milestones are known of an estimated 86 installed originally.*

At its maximum, the Minehead Turnpike Trust was responsible for roads between Minehead and Nether Stowey; Bishops Lydeard; Elsworthy, and Bampton. The era of Turnpike Trusts came to an end in 1888 when a Local Government Act gave responsibility for maintaining main roads to county councils and county borough councils.

South of Timberscombe, the land is primarily pasture with woodlands on some of the steeper slopes. Further east, the high land of Croydon Hill is largely covered by forestry plantations of mainly coniferous species. Alongside the tracks and in clearings, the former heathland vegetation is still present.

F21 *Devon cattle on Timberscombe Common. Like many former commons on Exmoor, this common has been enclosed and is now privately-owned farmland.*

On damp days in autumn, small cobwebs can become coated in dew. In close up, the effect is particularly beautiful with small droplets spaced along the fine silk fibres. Each droplet acts as a small lens to view the mosses beneath the web.

F22 and F23 Broadwood and Withycombe

A small plantation of Douglas fir to the north of Broadwood Farm includes the two tallest trees in England. One was measured at 61.3 metres (210 feet) in 2011 and another at 61.2 metres in 2017. For comparison, Nelson's Column in Trafalgar Square, London, is 169 feet (51.5 metres). The tallest tree in Britain is a Douglas fir growing in Reelig Glen near Inverness. It was measured at 66.4 metres (217 feet) in 2014.

The Douglas fir originates from the west coast of America and the tallest in the world is in Oregon. It was measured at 327 feet (99.6 metres) in 2008, so there is still some way to go for the Dunster trees. Once mature, Douglas firs tend to grow in girth rather than in height.

F23 *A tree on Oak Lane leading to the farm at Oak west of Withycombe. It ought to be an oak and, pleasingly, it is! The farmhouse at Oak is late sixteenth to early seventeenth century in origin.*

[Left] **F22** *England's tallest tree – a Douglas fir on the road to Broadwood Farm south of Dunster. The person in the picture is 5 feet 4 inches (1.6 metres) making the tree 38 times taller!*

G07 and G08 Red Gate and Shoulsbury Castle

Red Gate lies on the western boundary of the National Park between Fullaford Down and Wallover Down.

G07 *The gate at Red Gate is nothing special – not even a spot of red paint!.*

G07 *More interestingly, there is a stone to the west of Red Gate marking the boundary between the parishes of Brayford to the south and Challacombe to the north.*

Further east, the land rises to Shoulsbarrow Common. A large nearly square earthwork with rounded corners known as Shoulsbury Castle is situated above a steep slope to the south of the common. Local folklore suggests that Alfred held it against the Danes although the origins and purpose of the structure aren't clear. Most opinion seems to be that it is probably late Iron Age.[1]

The eastern boundary of Shoulsbarrow Common is close to the county boundary between Devon and Somerset and the boundary of the Exmoor Forest. An inscribed stone with the inscription *"to Christian Slowly, Lady of the Manor of Gratton, and to William …, Lord of the Manor of High Bray"* marks the boundary and is dated 1742.

G08 *The Sloley, or should it be 'Slowly'(?), Stone on the county boundary between Devon and Somerset, and the boundary of the former Exmoor Forest.*

G08 *A panoramic view showing the earthworks of Shoulsbury Castle from the north-east corner.*

G09 Mole's Chamber and Setta Barrow

Legend has it that the mysterious Mole's Chamber is named after a farmer called Mole who entered the mire at the site for a wager and disappeared into the bog complete with his horse.

G09 *Setta Barrow sits on the boundary of the Royal Forest and the Devon/Somerset county boundary. A Bronze Age bowl barrow with a mound surrounded by a ditch, Setta Barrow is unusual in still having part of a retaining kerb of stones around its base[1].*

G09 *Landscape north of Mole's Chamber.*

G10 Cornham Ford

West of Simonsbath, the River Barle descends through Cornham Ford. A tranquil area today, the valleys of the Barle and Burcombe were the centre of mining activity during a short time in the nineteenth century. Commencing in 1855, when mineral rights were sold by Frederic Knight to the Dowlais Iron Company of South Wales, early promise declined and work ceased by around 1860 after 175 tons of iron ore had been extracted. The workings were given the name 'Roman Adit' as they were on the site of supposed 'ancient' workings attributed to the Romans. However, these were probably sixteenth or seventeenth century. At Cornham Ford, there are remains of a row of six miners' cottages plus a mine office; several mine adits; the pit for a water wheel constructed to pump water from the mines, and a spoil heap from the nineteenth-century workings.

South of Cornham Ford and close to the approaching track that descends Burcombe from Blue Gate, there is an impressive set of mineral workings known as 'Roman Lode'. Excavations have established an earliest radiocarbon date to the mid Bronze Age. It is possible that copper or pigments or quartz were being exploited here prior to iron working and, if that is the case, it is also conceivable that iron was extracted here throughout the Iron Age, Roman and early medieval periods as well. Certainly, the size and complexity of the workings indicate that a long period of exploitation occurred here. The form of the openwork itself suggests a medieval or early post-medieval date, and it is likely that the majority of the workings date to this period[1].

G10 *View down Burcombe valley towards Cornham Ford. The traces of nineteenth-century iron ore mining are evident in the valley.*

G10
Entrance to a nineteenth-century mining adit at Cornham.

G10 *View along 'Roman Lode' where evidence of mineral extraction dates back to the Bronze Age.*

G11 Simonsbath and the Royal Forest

From Cornham, the River Barle descends Cornham Brake to Simonsbath in the heart of the Exmoor Forest.

In 1653, James Boevey purchased the freehold of the former Royal Forest of Exmoor in Somerset from Cromwell's Commonwealth government. The following year, James Boevey built the first house on the desolate moorland, at a central spot called Simonsbath. At the restoration of the Crown in 1660, freehold of the Forest reverted to the Crown and James Butler, 1st Duke of Ormond was named Keeper of Exmoor Forest as one of his many responsibilities in the court of Charles II. The Duke leased the Forest to James Boevey, who became chief forester and continued to live on Exmoor until 1670. A series of foresters undertook local management until the sale of the Forest by the Crown in 1818.

Exmoor Forest was disafforested by Act of Parliament in 1815. The land was divided up into a series of allotments with some allocated to those who had benefitted from rights over the Forest. An allotment of 12/22nds was retained by the Crown. The total area estimated at the time was 20,014 acres. The King's Allotment was 10,262 acres, that to Sir Thomas Acland was 3201 acres and 1880 acres were allotted to Sir Charles W, Bampfylde, with the remainder allotted to a series of other rights holders.

The King's Allotment was put up for sale to the highest bidder in June 1818 and the highest tender of £50,000 was received from John Knight of Wolverley Hall, Worcestershire. The conveyance of the sale was not completed until March 1820 by which time, John Knight had also purchased Sir Thomas Acland's and Sir Charles Bampfylde's allotments. Subsequent purchases took John Knight's total ownership of the former Exmoor Forest to 16,128 acres.

In the 1820's 'reclamation' of the Forest began:

- 22 miles (35 kilometres) of roads were built on existing tracks to link Simonsbath with Exford and Lynton via Brendon (John Knight lived in Lynton in the 1820s at what became the Castle Hotel).
- A 29 mile (46 kilometre) boundary wall was constructed around John Knight's Forest acquisitions with double-gates at roads to prevent stock straying e. g. Brendon Two Gates and Honeymead Two Gates.
- Large sections of the Prayway and Warren canals covering nearly 10 miles (15km) were constructed (but never completed).
- Pinkery Pond was constructed – see **E09**.
- Active land cultivation started and, by 1845, around 2500 acres (1000 hectares) had been ploughed.
- The first farms were formed at Cornham and Honeymead. At this time John Knight did not attempt to establish tenanted farms but kept Exmoor 'in hand'.

G11 *River Barle above Simonsbath at Cornham Brake.*

In 1841 John Knight retired to Italy and his son Frederic took over. John Knight had created farms at Cornham, Honeymead and the home farm at Simonsbath Barton in the 1820s to enable him to manage the estate. His son, Frederic, however, needed income from the estate and set about letting the existing farms, creating new ones and looking at other opportunities to generate income, such as mining.

Honeymead Farm was let on Lady Day 1842 and Simonsbath Barton was let in 1843. Frederic Knight created further farms at Red Deer Farm (later Gallon House); Emmett's Grange (let in 1844 with 1300 acres); Wintershead, Horsen and Crooked Post let in 1844; Warren built in the winter 1844/5; Duredon and Larkbarrow **(E14)** let in 1846, and Driver in 1847. Pinkery, Titchcombe and Cornham Hill were dedicated as farms in 1847 but built later, and Tom's Hill in 1850.

The new farms were based on 50 acre enclosures in the valleys, surrounded with stone and earth banks 4 feet high, topped with 2 feet of turf and planted with beech hedges. A beech tree nursery was established just north of Simonsbath to supply hedge plants and, in 1850, a considerable sum at the time of £16 was paid for a supply of beech nuts.

In April 1886, Frederic Knight sold the reversion of the whole of the Exmoor and Brendon estates totalling 21,893 acres (8860 hectares) to Earl Fortescue and his son Viscount Ebrington for £193,060. The whole estate passed to Viscount Ebrington (later 4th Earl) on 12 January 1898. The Fortescue family retained ownership until the 1980s.

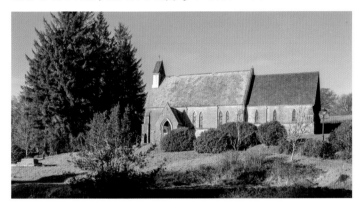

G11 *At the sale of Exmoor Forest in 1820 the land was 'extraparochial', as it did not lie within any established parish. However, 12 acres was retained by the Crown for a church, parsonage and homestead if the former Forest should ever become established as a civil and ecclesiastical parish. The land was made available in 1856, when formal establishment of a parish took place, and St Luke's church was constructed at around that time.*

G11 *Royal Marines running through Simonsbath on their 1664 challenge in 2014. The challenge was to mark the 350th anniversary of the formation of the Marines in 1664 by skiing 1664km, sailing 1664km, cycling 1664km, canoeing 193km and finally running 1664km.*

G11 Ashcombe Gardens

On acquiring the Royal Forest, John Knight developed plans to build a mansion and landscaped gardens at the rear of Simonsbath House. The Mansion was never completed and much of the structure was pulled down in 1895. However, the traces of the gardens in Ashcombe and a small cottage do remain, although much altered. White Rock cottages were built in February 1820 as two, two-room semi-detached cottages, probably to house a gardener and other estate staff.

In 1857, parts of the two cottages began to be used as a school and the buildings were subsequently extended becoming a primary school from 1958 until it closed in 1970. After the school closed in 1970, the buildings at White Rocks were used for around twenty years as a Field Centre, before falling into disuse and suffering deterioration. In 2013 the building was protected to allow archaeological investigation and eventual consolidation or restoration.

[Above] **G11** *Other reminders of the former gardens include the remains of a leat system that might have channelled water to a waterfall feature.*

G11 *Mysterious chambers below White Rocks cottages and close to the stream are thought to have been cold stores.*

[Left] **G11** *The approach to the former landscaped gardens at Ashcombe, Simonsbath, are flanked by two large natural outcrops of quartz known as 'White Rocks.'*

G12 *A view of the remains of Wheal Eliza Mine alongside the River Barle south of Simonsbath.*

G12 Wheal Eliza

Wheal Eliza Mine (originally called Wheal Maria) was first worked for copper from 1845-54, then iron until 1857. Various trial adits were dug before two main shafts were excavated to a depth of some 300 feet (100 metres). These were pumped out by machinery powered from a waterwheel on the south side of the river, supplied by two leats running back up the valley.

On the north side of the River Barle, platforms and rectangular enclosures are visible, along with the footings of several buildings, presumably the cottages built here for the miners, or the blacksmiths and carpenters' shops and Account House, which were completed in 1846. The workings were not successful due to insufficient ore and by 1858 the mine had been abandoned and allowed to flood.

Wheal Eliza was the setting for a very sad story in 1858, shortly after its abandonment, when the area became notorious for the murder of a seven-year-old girl, Anna Maria Burgess. On the death of their mother, two older children went into domestic service on a farm in North Molton and Anna moved with her father, William Burgess, into lodgings at Gallon House Cot in Simonsbath.

The Reverend W. H. Thornton (1830-1916), who had been recently installed as the first vicar of Exmoor, helped raise money to support Burgess, but this was spent on alcohol. In June 1858,

Burgess left his lodgings with his daughter, telling the landlady that he was taking Anna to live with her grandmother in Porlock Weir. However, the remains of burnt clothes were found which had belonged to Anna, and investigations in Porlock Weir prompted by the Reverend Thornton, established that the little girl had not been taken there.

Thornton suspected murder and instigated a search for Anna. In the meantime, Burgess had escaped by boat to Swansea but was found and brought back to Simonsbath and was imprisoned in Dulverton. He said nothing about the whereabouts of his daughter and searches of the local moors continued for two months. A witness then came forward and said he had seen Burgess one night near the Wheal Eliza Mine. Local magistrates ordered the 100-metre mineshaft to be drained which took until November and cost £350. Once the water had been pumped away, a bag was found containing Anna's remains. Burgess was found guilty of murder and, before being hanged, he admitted that he had killed Anna so that he could spend the 2s 6d (12.5 pence) a week intended for her welfare on drink. He was taken to the gaol in Taunton and hanged on 4 January 1859.[2]

Anna Maria's grave can be seen at St Luke's parish church in Simonsbath.

G13 *As its name suggests, Honeymead Two Gates was originally the location for double gates on the new road from Exford to Simonsbath built by John Knight in the 1820s to serve his new estate on the former Royal Forest.*

G13 *Gallon House was named Red Deer Farm when it was built by Frederic Knight in around 1840. As well as farming, the house was used at times as an Inn.*

G14 *A small hut at Newlands Farm is sited opposite a large complex of limestone quarries and lime kilns active in the latter part of the nineteenth century. Limestone occurs on Exmoor as outcrops within the Ilfracombe Slate beds running east-west in a broad band from Combe Martin through Simonsbath, Exford and Treborough.*

G14 *The well-named 'Silly Bridge' over the still small River Exe west of Exford is not for the faint-hearted. You only know it's possible to drive across because the car in front managed it without incident!*

G15 Exford

The Domesday Book of 1086 records eight settlements in Exford parish, five called Exford and the others at Almesworthy (Edmunds homestead), Stone and Downscombe. In the mid nineteenth century there were several iron and copper mines in and around the village operated by the Exford Iron Ore Co. The Devon & Somerset Staghounds have had their kennels, built by Montague Bissett, at Exford since 1875.[2]

G15 *The church, dedicated to St Mary Magdalene (formerly known as the church of St Salvyn), has a tower dating from the fifteenth century. The south aisle probably dates from 1542, however the nave, chancel and porch were not built until 1867. The church was restored in 1893.*

G15 *Exford bridge was rebuilt in 1930, designed by Edward Stead, County Surveyor. It is on a medieval site but it is not known to what extent it contains earlier fabric.*

G15 *The Exmoor White Horse Inn is featured on the Exford Tithe Map of 1840.*

G15 *A medieval screen that had been removed from the church of St Audries, West Quantoxhead (now demolished) and stored in a barn, was reassembled in Exford church in 1929.[1 and 2]*

G16 and G17 Stone, Kitnor Heath and Holloway Lane

Stone lies to the east of Exford. It was a small Saxon estate held by a man called Brictric in 1066 and, twenty years later, by Roger de Courcelles, who held many manors in the area. The present building is shown as a country house on Day and Musters map of Somerset 1782 and is an unusually fine house for the period on Exmoor. It belonged to Sir Thomas Dyke Acland, the last Warden of Exmoor Forest, whose Crown Lease expired in 1814.

G16 *The eighteenth-century Stone country house.*

Prescott Down, Stone Down and Kitnor Heath are to the north of Stone. Kitnor refers to the Kite, a bird of prey that was once very numerous in Britain. Persecution in the nineteenth century led to its near extinction and there were only around 80 pairs in Wales in 1992. Subsequent conservation efforts increased the numbers in Wales and reintroductions have helped expand the range to include much of central England centred on the Chilterns. Despite regular visits by Kites to Exmoor, this bird has not yet re-established itself as a breeding bird in the National Park.

G17 *Holloway Lane descends towards Codsend, a seventeenth-century euphemism for God's-End, meaning 'isolated and bleak.'*[4]

G18 Luckwell Bridge

G18 *'K6' telephone box at Luckwell Bridge. The K6 (kiosk number six) was designed by Giles Gilbert Scott for the General Post Office to commemorate the Silver Jubilee of the coronation of King George V in 1935 and became the most widely deployed kiosk in the UK.*[1&2]

G18 *Long Lane heading south to Luckwell Bridge.*

G19 Cutcombe and Wheddon Cross

The settlement at Cutcombe dates back at least a thousand years and is called Udecombe in the Domesday Book of 1086.[4]

G19 Exmoor's main livestock market is based at Wheddon Cross and is operated by Exmoor Farmers Livestock Auctions Ltd. The company was established in 1997 when local farmers came together to buy shares so that the livestock market could be purchased and continue to operate when it was threatened with closure. The current modern facilities were developed in 2010/11 to ensure a long-term future for the market.

[Above and top right] **G19** *St John's church, Cutcombe, dates to the late thirteenth century and was extensively restored in the 1862. The base of the font is Norman.[1]*

G20 *View north of Stowey Farm with Stowey Ball hill on the right and Dunkery Hill in the distance on the left. 'Ball' is the name given to many rounded hills on Exmoor.*

G20 Stowey, Kersham and Putham Woods

G20 *An early nineteenth century Chargot estate cottage at Couple Cross. Several similar cottages were built around the estate including another in Kingsbridge, Luxborough (H22).*

G20 *The ruins of Stowey Mill on the boundary between Kersham and Putham woods. The mill is recorded on Cutcombe Tithe Map and Apportionment Book of 1842 and Robert Sedgebeer is thought to be the last miller, operating there from at least 1877 until around 1886. He lived there with his wife Ann and eight children. Robert was said to be an alcoholic who rode to Timberscombe every evening and, after a night of drinking, his friends threw him over his horse which brought him home.[1]*

G21 *Some of the overgrown ruins from the small settlement at Clicket, abandoned in 1890.*

G21 The Lost Village of Clicket

The Lost Village of Clicket is located on a public footpath which runs along a small valley to the south of Croydon House, Timberscombe. It is very easy to miss, as the various ruins of houses, a farm, a mill, quarries and limekilns are very overgrown. Although the village of Clicket may have existed as early as the 1300s, it doesn't definitely appear in records until 1809 and was never a large settlement.

In the 1881 census there were 20 people listed as living there in three families. The last baby to be born at Clicket was Lily Burge (later Bryant), who was born in 1889 (she died in 1977 in Bristol). In 1890, Clicket was abandoned because there was no employment left (the quarry and mill had closed), farming was in a depression and, with no road access, the village was too inaccessible.[16]

G22 and G23 **Withycombe Common and Rodhuish**

In the north-eastern corner of the National Park, between Dunster and Luxborough, Croydon and Black Hills extend to over 350 metres (1,148 feet) in height. The climate here is relatively dry and these hills are covered in heathland, rather than the wetter moorland typical of the high ground to the south and west of Exmoor. Conifer plantations cover large areas of former heathland, although open heathland remains on Black Hill and Rodhuish Common.

G22 The triangulation (trig) point on Withycombe Common sits upon the largest of a group of three Bronze Age barrows running north to south at the summit of Black Hill.

G22 St Bartholomew's church, Rodhuish, is a former chapel of ease of fifteenth or sixteenth century date. It was restored in 1826 and 1924. The Norman font was moved from Carhampton church in the nineteenth century.[1]

G23 Exmoor ponies grazing on Rodhuish Common, with Black Hill in the background.

G24 and G25 Roadwater and Beggearn Huish

Roadwater was formerly known as *Rode,* and had a mill by 1243. Rode or Rod is Old English for rood or cross and it is likely that the name was derived from a cross by a stream. During the eighteenth and nineteenth centuries, there were a large number of mills set beside the Washford River.

G24 *Oatway Cottage, Roadwater, originated in a late medieval hall house and was altered in the seventeenth, eighteenth, nineteenth and twentieth centuries.[1]*

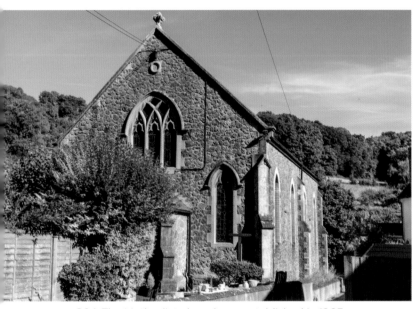

G24 *Though being a substantial structure with 60 cm thick brick and concrete walls and concrete roof, the First World War pillbox on the southern approach to Roadwater was disguised as a timber-roofed shed. The roof was restored with fibreglass waterproofing in 2008 after the original lead flashing was stolen!*

G24 *The Methodist chapel was established in 1907.*

G25 *A view of the landscape south of Beggearn Huish. Beggearn is thought to mean 'beyond the family allotment' from the Old English, Begeondan, meaning beyond and Huish from Old English 'hiwisc' which means household.[4]*

H08 Muxworthy and Sherracombe

Muxworthy is a farm on the western boundary of the National Park. The name is from the Old English meaning Muc's settlement.

Archaeological investigations of earthworks at Sherracombe Ford have shown them to be made up from the waste resulting from iron smelting. Evidence, such as pottery remains and radiocarbon dating, indicates that the site was in intensive use for around 100 years from sometime after 50 AD to 150 AD – the early period of Roman occupation in Britain.[20] Iron ore is not found in the immediate vicinity but there are iron mines nearby, including the so-called 'Roman Lode' at Burcombe **(G10)**.

H08 *Kedworthy Combe near Muxworthy.*

[Far left] **H08** *Archaeological dig in progress in 2002 at Sherracombe Ford.*

H08 *View towards Muxworthy from Muxworthy Lane.*

H09 **Five Burrows Hill and Comerslade**

A Bronze Age barrow cemetery on Five Burrows Hill is actually a grouping of nine Bronze Age barrows dating from between 4500 to 2700 years ago.[1]

H09 *One of the largest of the nine barrows on Five Burrows Hill.*

H09 *A sense of the extent of the former Royal Forest can be gained from this panoramic view of Comerslade.*

H10 and H11 Emmett's Grange and Wintershead

Emmett's Grange and Wintershead are two of the Knight farms established in the mid 1800s as part of the agricultural improvement of the former Royal Forest (see pages 98 and 99). A Neolithic flint implement was found in July 1919 on Wintershead Farm. It is a well patinated flake three inches in length and of triangular cross-section, with a dorsal ridge; it has secondary chipping along one edge. It is now in Taunton Museum.[1]

H10 *Emmett's Grange is the best of the surviving Knight farm buildings in the former Royal Forest.*

H11 *Wintershead Farm above Kinsford Water, with Long Holcombe hill to the left.*

H12 Cow Castle

H12 *Cow Castle is a hilltop enclosure probably of Iron Age date with a single defensive rampart. It dominates the Barle valley, being sited to the south of Simonsbath on a steep-sided isolated knoll at the confluence of the River Barle with White Water.*

H13 and H14 **Landacre**

Landacre was proposed as a possible location for a large drinking water reservoir in the late 1960s. Had that development gone ahead it would have had a considerable impact on the area, leading to the bridge being submerged and Cow Castle, upstream, becoming an island – see page 164.

H14 *Moorland at Landacre Lane.*

H13 *Landacre Bridge is probably late medieval in origin. The current structure is the result of restoration in 1875.*

H15 Court Hill, Location for the Exford Show

Court Hill is topped by the Bronze Age Hernes Barrow, which was called Ernesburg and Hernesbureghe in the 1219 and 1279 perambulations of Exmoor forest.[1]

The Exford Show, hosted by the Devon & Somerset Staghounds and the Exmoor Pony Society, takes place at Court Hill in August.

A serious business! Uniquely, the Exford Show includes judging of cast antlers from Exmoor red deer, reflecting the importance of red deer in Exmoor's culture (see page 72).

Sheep classes are held for the two local breeds, Exmoor Horn (see page 82) and, in this case, Devon Closewool. The breed arose around the mid-1800s when Exmoor Horn sheep were crossed with Devon Longwools. The resultant, intermediate-sized, sheep proved very popular and expanded rapidly in numbers. The Devon Closewool Sheep Breeders Society was formed in 1923.[17]

Better luck next year!.

Looks scary, but a clear round in the show jumping!

Starting early in life – a young entrant in the pony competition.

The Exmoor Pony Society co-hosts the Exford Show. The Society was set up in 1921 for the registration of pure-bred Exmoor ponies; the conservation of the breed, and the preservation of the breed standard – see page 130.[18]

Exmoor Pony Society judging underway.

H16 *View of Exe valley from Higher Combe.*

H17 **Staddon Hill and Larcombe Foot**

H17 *The small Iron Age camp at Staddon Hill sits in a clearing in the forestry plantation.*

H17 *Kemps Lane descends from Staddon Hill to Larcombe Foot.*

H17 *The River Exe at Larcombe Foot.*

H18 Ison Lane and Nurcott

Ison Lane runs from Oldrey to Nurcott just north of Winsford. Ison is from the German Eisen, meaning iron. In Elizabethan times, miners came to Exmoor from the Harz region of Germany to work in local mines.[4]

H18 *Great Nurcott from East Nurcott with Bye Common behind.*

H18 *Lee Farm viewed from Ison Lane.*

H19 and H20 **Quarme Combe and Lype Hill**

The name of the River Quarme is derived from Old English 'awne' meaning water or river.[4]

H19 *View from Quarme Combe to Dunkery.*

H20 *View north from Lype Break.*

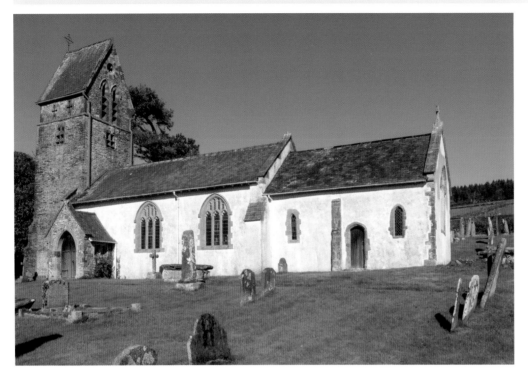

Luxborough is divided into the hamlets of Churchtown, Kingsbridge and Pooltown, which lie within a mile of each other. Luxborough, 'Loloches-berie' in the Domesday Book, means 'stronghold or hill of a man called Lulluc.[2]

H21 *St Mary's church at Churchtown, Luxborough, has a thirteenth-century chancel and a fifteenth-century tower with upper stages added in 1861. Most of the nave, the north aisle and south porch date to the nineteenth century. The shaft of a fourteenth-century cross stands in the churchyard. The gabled tower is an unusual feature shared by Stoke Pero* **(E16)** *and Wootton Courtenay* **(E19)** *churches on Exmoor.*

H21 *Chargot House was built in 1826 for John Lethbridge. A three-light stained glass window in St Mary's church commemorates B. E. Lethbridge who was killed in 1899 during the South African Wars.[1]*

H21 *The ponds below Chargot House are referred to as fishponds in the Luxborough Tithe Map of 1843.[1]*

H22 Luxborough – Kingsbridge and Pooltown

H22 *Landscape to the east of Luxborough with Kingsbridge and Perley Wood on the left, and Druid's Combe Wood top middle and right.*

H22 *Seventeenth century estate cottages in Kingsbridge, Luxborough. A similar building is at Couple Cross* **(G20)**.

H23 Treborough

The name Treborough is thought to be derived from the Celtic 'treberg' meaning 'hamlet by the waterfall', or 'wooded place or hill', from the Old English 'treow' for tree.[4]

H23 *Langridge Wood is mostly recent conifer plantation on a probable ancient woodland site. Within the wood is a prehistoric stone cist dating to the Bronze Age. The cairn above the cist was removed for road material in 1820 and the cist was found to contain a skeleton which was removed and reinterred at Treborough churchyard.*

Interior of the Bronze Age burial cist.

H23 *St Peter's church, Treborough, is mostly late fifteenth or early sixteenth century, with some fourteenth-century work. It was restored in the early nineteenth century.*

H23 *Early nineteenth-century lime kilns near Treborough Quarries. Slate and building stone were extracted from the quarries for around 500 years, not closing fully until 1938. The Ilfracombe Slates are quite waved on the surface, but sufficient for roofing, doorsteps, cisterns and flooring. The quarry provided slate for Dunster Castle in 1426.[1]*

H24 **Leighland Chapel**

H24 *Leighland Chapel is a small settlement set on a ridge above a tributary of the Washford River.*

[Left] **H24** *St Giles church at Leighland Chapel was built in 1861-2 on the site of a medieval chapel. [Right]* **H24** *The hamlet at Lower Hayne with two cottages dating back to the seventeenth century.*

H25 Nettlecombe Court

H25 *View of Nettlecombe Park from Beacon Hill above Sticklepath.*

Nettlecombe was originally Netelcumbe meaning the place or valley where the nettles grow.

Nettlecombe Court has never been bought or sold. It was held before the Norman Conquest by Prince Godwine, son of King Harold, and William the Conqueror assumed possession of Nettlecombe after defeating King Harold at the Battle of Hastings. In 1160, Henry II granted Nettlecombe to Hugh de Raleigh, and to his heirs in perpetuity. It passed

H25 *Nettlecombe Court buildings from the south east with St Mary's church and walled gardens behind.*

to Warine de Ralegh and on through direct blood heirs until the nineteenth century. In 1848, the estate became a seat of the Trevelyan baronets by the marriage of Sir John Trevilian to Lady Whalesborough, heiress of Nettlecombe via her Ralegh maternal line. Nettlecombe was then held in continuity by Trevelyan successors until the twentieth century, at the death of Joan Trevelyan and her husband Garnet Wolsey, and their descendants are still here.

The house became a boarding school for girls in the late 1950s and, since 1967, it has been the home of the Leonard Wills Field Centre run by the Field Studies Council, an educational charity.

Nettlecombe oaks: several sessile oaks in Nettlecombe Park are outstandingly large and were famous from ancient accounts for their great size. Nettlecombe oaks once provided timber for shipbuilding including to help build the ships of the English fleet that defeated the Spanish Armada in 1588. In the nineteenth century, very good prices were offered to the Trevelyan baronet to cut down and sell the great oaks, but he left them standing and the trees have been protected ever since. Some have now grown to a girth of 23 feet (7.0 m). Today, Nettlecombe acorns are sold to nurseries to grow new sapling oak trees.[2]

H25 *A row of splendid veteran oaks in the grounds at Nettlecombe. (Photograph taken with permission.)*

H26 Monksilver and Combe Sydenham

The name of the village means monk's wood. In the Domesday Book it was simply Selvre, from the Latin 'silva' for a wood, although it has also been suggested that Sulfhere, in AD 897, referred to the silvery stream below the village.

In 1113, the manor was given by Robert de Chandos to endow Goldcliff Priory, which he had just established near Newport in Monmouthshire. In 1441, it passed with the priory to Tewkesbury Abbey and then, in 1474, to the canons of Windsor. In the fourteenth century the name changed to "Monksilver".[2]

H26 *All Saints parish church dates back to the twelfth century with a window of that period. The tower is fourteenth century and in the fifteenth century a stair turret was added to the tower, the porch was reconstructed, chancel widened, nave rebuilt, south aisle and chapel added. The church was restored between 1843 and 1863 when the tower was crenellated.*

H26 *The woods at Bird's Hill south-west of Monksilver are carpeted with bluebells in the spring.*

H26 *Now unused and partially hidden by overgrowth, the former Wesleyan Methodist chapel at Monksilver was supplied by W. Harbrow of South Bermondsey Station, London, and is another example of a 'Tin Tabernacle' similar to that at Porlock Weir (**(C16)**).*

H26 *To the south of Monksilver, is the estate at Combe Sydenham with a manor house that dates to the late fifteenth or early sixteenth century. In 1585, Admiral Sir Francis Drake married Elizabeth Sydenham, the only child and sole heiress of Sir George Sydenham. However, before the marriage took place, Drake left on a long voyage. In Drake's absence, Elizabeth's father arranged for her to be married instead to a son of the Wyndham family of nearby Orchard Wyndham. Tradition states that, on the wedding day as the couple approached the church of St Mary at Stogumber, a loud clap of thunder was heard and a large meteorite crashed through the roof. This was seen as a bad omen and the wedding was cancelled. Drake had arrived back in Plymouth on that same day, and he and Elizabeth were later married at the church of All Saints in Monksilver. The 14-inch (360 mm) diameter meteorite, known as "Drake's cannon ball", has remained at the house ever since.[2]*

108 *Small hamlet at Holewater close to the south-west boundary of the National Park..*

109 *The landscape at Lyddicombe. The combe drains into the River Mole that flows south-westwards to South Molton where it joins the Yeo. Mole is from the Celtic 'moel' meaning bare, rounded summit which describes the origin of the river west of Sandyway Cross.*

109 *Sign of the remote Poltimore Arms. Like a significant number of properties across the National Park, the pub is not connected to mains electricity.*

110 *View to Fyldon Common from Fyldon Hill.*

I11 and I12 **Long Holcombe and Sherdon**

I11 *Long Holcombe fell within the part of the Royal Forest purchased by John Knight in 1820. The stream in the valley, Kinsford Water, joins Sherdon Water and flows on to the River Barle.*

I11 *Remnant beech hedge near Long Holcombe Cross.*

I11 *The stone-faced bank at Long Holcombe is part of the Forest boundary.*

I12 *Sherdon Farm was probably constructed in the early 1800s. It lies within the former Royal Forest and is in Exmoor parish but is on an allotment of land that was not acquired by John Knight.*

The Exmoor Pony

The UK has 14 native horse and pony breeds, of which 12, including the Exmoor pony, are considered rare according to the Rare Breeds Survival Trust (RBST)[19].

Exmoor ponies have been on the moor since ancient times and have adapted to survive on low quality moorland grazing. This environment shaped their size, characteristic hardiness, independent spirit and native intelligence.[18] The Exmoor Pony Society was formed in 1921 and maintains the studbook for the breed. The majority of the breed is made up from domesticated ponies but the moorland herds have an important part to play in maintaining bloodlines and the hardiness of the breed. Each year, the Society attends shows to promote the breed, including the Exford Show in August – see pages 116-117. Exmoor ponies are bay, brown and dun in colour and carry characteristic mealy markings on the muzzle and around the eye and flanks. The resemblance of the breed to primitive wild horses is often noted and their distinctive appearance, together with their hardiness, has made them popular in conservation grazing programmes around the UK and in mainland Europe.

The ponies on moorland areas are rounded up each year to check their health – see page 35. Many of the foals are sold on to new owners but the large-scale horse markets, such as Bampton Fair, that once provided a market for the ponies are no longer held.

'King of the castle'.

Inquisitive Exmoor pony foals on Anstey Common.

An Exmoor pony in the Valley of Rocks, Lynton. In areas like this, that are popular with the public, it is common for people to start feeding ponies with 'treats' such as sugar cubes, bread and carrots. Unfortunately, rather than being kind, this is extremely harmful to Exmoor ponies that are adapted to thrive on low nutrient forage. An over-rich diet, high in sugars and starches, can lead to painful inflammation called laminitis in the tissues of the pony's hooves. Once initiated, the condition is very hard to treat and the pony can become lame and, in bad cases, have to be put down. So please – do not feed!

[Facing page] Herds of semi-feral free-ranging ponies are still a common sight on moorland across Exmoor. This group on Brendon Common are in their thick winter coats.

113 **Withypool Common**

Withypool Common survives as a common after applications for enclosure in 1869 and 1879 were rejected.[8]

113 *The Bronze Age barrow with a triangulation (trig) point provides a prominent landmark at the summit of Withypool Common. This is the most intact of the Brightworthy Barrows, a series of three barrows that formed a line roughly east to west.*

113 *The Brightworthy Barrows were excavated for road stone in 1913, and the remains of the middle of the three barrows can just be made out. Unfortunately, nothing remains of the third barrow.*

113 *Exmoor ponies at Sherdon Rock overlooking the Barle valley.*

Invasive signal crayfish

The signal crayfish was introduced in the 1970s from North America as a commercial food species, but soon escaped from commercial fisheries. Unfortunately, signal crayfish are carriers of crayfish plague and outcompete the native white-clawed crayfish for habitat and food. As a result, the presence of signal crayfish is often quickly followed by the decline and extinction of the native crayfish species. In addition, signal crayfish are considered a serious threat to other wildlife in the river, as the crayfish reach considerable numbers and have a ferocious appetite, feeding on invertebrates and the eggs and young of important fish such as salmon and trout.

I14 *A track between small irregular fields at Brightworthy. This was named Brizenesworthy in 1298 – the settlement of someone called Britsten.*[4]

Signal crayfish are considerably larger than the native crayfish, with males up to 16cm in body length and females up to 12cm. They can be recognised by the whitish patch at the joint between the two fingers of the claw, which they open wide to "signal" to other crayfish. The underside of their claws is brick red.

A survey of the River Barle in 2014 showed that signal crayfish had colonised the river to a stretch just upstream of Withypool. Following this discovery, an innovative project has been undertaken to try and control the numbers of the invasive species and prevent further colonisation upstream. The technique used is to capture signal crayfish in traps and remove all but the largest males. The large males then have two of their rear appendages removed so that they cannot breed, and are released back into the river. The sterilised males continue to feed, including taking small specimens of their own species, but don't reproduce. Initial results indicate that the approach is being successful. However, the programme will need to be maintained to be effective in the longer term because it is not possible to eradicate the species entirely, and the male crayfish grow back the mating appendages when they next moult, so have to be caught and treated again.

I14 *Knighton Combe on Withypool Common. Knighton is from Old English Cnid meaning the farm of a young warrior or royal retainer.*[4]

I15 Withypool

Withy is a name for willow trees, hence 'pool by willows'.

[Right] I15 *The Royal Oak Inn was constructed in the late 1600s. Apparently, R. D. Blackmore wrote part of Lorna Doone in the bar, and artist Alfred Munnings had a studio in the loft. In the 1930s, the inn was owned by Gwladys and Maxwell Knight, a spy master and radio broadcaster upon whom Ian Fleming based the character of James Bond's boss, M. During the Second World War, Woolacombe beach in North Devon was used to simulate the invasion of Normandy and General Dwight Eisenhower is said to have planned some of the operation from the Royal Oak.*[2]

I15 *Withypool Bridge is relatively modern, built to replace an earlier bridge some 100 metres upstream.*

I16 and I17 **Winsford Hill and The Punchbowl**

Winsford Hill is composed of Pickwell Down Sandstone, a Devonian rock younger than the Great Hangman Sandstone of the Exmoor coast and laid down some 370 to 360 million years ago in shallow seas, tidal lagoons and deltas.

I16 A group of three Bronze Age barrows known as Wambarrows are located on the summit of Winsford Hill. They are better preserved than the similar group of three at Brightworthy Barrows on Withypool Common **(I13)**. *The barrows are mentioned in Exmoor Forest perambulations of 1219 and 1279 as 'Wamburg' and 'Wimbureghe' respectively.[1]*

I17 An intriguing landform known as 'The Punchbowl' lies to the northern side of Winsford Hill. Although Exmoor is not thought to have had a covering of ice, even at the maximum extent of ice cover in the Ice Age, the shape of the Punchbowl looks very like that of a glacial 'corrie' that is formed when a permanent snow patch or small glacier settles within a hollow on the side of a slope.

I18 **Winsford**

Winsford probably dates from Saxon times when the settlement built up around the confluence of the River Exe and River Winn. It appears as Winesford in the Domesday Book of 1085.

I18 *The substantial parish church, with its tall, late fifteenth-century, tower, indicates that Winsford has been an important community since at least medieval times. The font has some fine Norman carving, the chancel is thirteenth century and there is a remnant of fourteenth-century stained glass in the east window[1].*

I18 *A 1609 panel with the Royal Coat of Arms of James I hangs inside Winsford church. At the time he acceded to the throne, James I of England was already James VI of Scotland and the two countries were united under his kingship. His Royal Coat of Arms merges badges and symbols from both coats of arms. During the English Civil War in the 1640s, insignia relating to the role of the royal family in the Church, particularly to the Stuarts, were targets for destruction. Thus, the Winsford panel is a rare survival and is said to be one of only four that still exist.*

I18 *The Royal Oak, Winsford, was formerly a sixteenth or seventeenth century farm-house that later became an inn.[1]*

[Facing page] 'A perfect English village'. View to Winsford on a bright day in May.

120 *Higher Thorn Close is a deserted medieval farm site mentioned in the lay subsidy of 1327. No clear remains of the farm are visible on the ground[1]. 'Close' means an enclosure from the Old French 'clos' and implies an early enclosure of land from the surrounding heath.*

121 *Bearland Wood Ventilation Chimney.*

The Brendon Hills lie to the east of Winsford. The hills provide an undulating landscape that is now permanent pasture and woodland but was the location of considerable industrial activity in the nineteenth century.

Langham Hill Pit was one of the Brendon Hills Iron Ore Company works and was started in 1839 when it was originally called 'Goosemoor Mine'. A pumping and winding engine and engine house were installed in 1866. Reduced demand due to cheaper imports of Spanish ore, caused the mine to close in 1874. It reopened in 1876, but little mine development took place and subsequent ore production may have used existing stocks. Mining at Langham Hill pit finally ceased by September 1883, along with all mining on the Brendons.[1]

To the west of Langham Hill, the Bearland Wood Ventilation Chimney was built in 1860 and is a rare survival of Welsh mining technology. Its purpose was to assist the ventilation of the iron mine workings below. The chimney (around 6 metres tall) was connected to the mine workings by a duct. A fire was lit on a grate within the chimney and the rising hot air from the fire drew stale air out of the mines through the duct from the mine workings, thus ensuring a flow of fresh air through the workings themselves. When, by 1864, no iron ore had been found in the Bearland Wood adit, the flue was abandoned.[21]

121 *A closer view of the chimney shows the access to the grate where a fire was lit to draw stale air from the mine workings below, allowing fresh air into the adit from its entrance.*

[Facing page] **121** *The conserved remains of the former nineteenth-century engine house at Langham Hill.*

122 and 123 Burrow Farm Engine House and the Naked Boy Stone

Travelling east from Wheddon Cross, the B3224 follows the ridge across the Brendon Hills. The land south of the ridge is mostly improved farmland with large fields and few features. To the north of the ridge, the landscape is more varied with steeper valleys, and woods and plantations, as well as farmland.

122 *View north from Cowleaze Copse. Until the 1950s and 1960s, many of the woods on Exmoor had been managed by periodic cutting in a system known as 'coppicing'. 'Copse' is a shortened version of the word. Many former coppice woodlands on Exmoor today have either been allowed to grow to mature oak and other broadleaved trees, or have been planted with conifers like this one at Cowleaze.*

Burrow Farm Mine, one of a number of mines built in the Brendon Hills iron field, was first sunk about 1860. The Cornish-style engine house was probably built in 1880 and housed a rotary beam engine serving the dual purpose of pumping and winding.[1]

[Left] 123 *To the east of Burrow Farm Mine, the Naked Boy Stone is a medieval boundary stone about 1.25 metres high, of undressed granite, marking the Old Cleeve and Brompton Regis parish boundary.[1]*

[Top left and facing page] 123 *Burrow Farm Engine House.*

124 West Somerset Mineral Line and Incline

The West Somerset Mineral Railway was built between 1857 and 1864 to export iron ore from the mines on the Brendon Hills. The most significant remains are those of the kilometre-long inclined plane that took the railway from the Brendon Hills, at over 380 metres above sea level, to Comberow, at around 150 metres. From Comberow, the line went to the harbour at Watchet West Pier, where the iron ore was loaded onto ships and transported across the Bristol Channel to Newport in South Wales for smelting at Ebbw Vale.

The Incline had two sets of standard gauge rails. At the summit of the incline, a winding house contained two large, cast iron, winding drums, that raised and lowered the wagons. The drums were circa 5.48 metres in diameter and 1 metre wide. Both were mounted on the same axle, which was supported on four wrought iron frames bolted to the floor. The incline cables, approximately 1000 metres long, unwound from the top of the west drum and the bottom of the east drum, passing through ducts to emerge between the rails near a brakehouse to the north. The incline was designed to operate on the 'self-acting' principle, whereby the heavier descending loads hauled up the empty ascending wagons. Following the closure of the mines in 1883, this was not possible and a small steam engine was installed to turn the drums. The railway closed in 1898, but reopened briefly from 1907 to 1909. The rails and metalwork were taken for the war effort in 1916, but the drums were too large to be dismantled and were blown up in situ, thereby demolishing most of the winding house.[1]

124 *The walls that can be seen today on the site of the cable winding house bear no resemblance to the original winding house building. They were built in 1942/3, when the landowner began converting the remains to agricultural use, by building new east and west walls with material from the demolition of the brake house and inserting windows from elsewhere. The mounds in the foreground are all that remains of miners' cottages built in the 1860s.*

124 *In two places, the trackbed of the incline is supported across gaps by stone bridges known as underbridges.*

124 and 125 Beulah Chapel and Ralegh's Cross

Work began at the Ralegh's Cross mine in 1852, and several hundred miners came from other parts (largely Cornwall) as mining expanded in the area. This led to the development of a sizable settlement, including around 60 cottages built for the miners' families. To complete the village there was an Anglican corrugated iron church, a shop, temperance house, reading room, a bank and Beulah Chapel, a Bible Christian chapel also used as a school. Some of these buildings remain in various states of preservation, although there is no trace of the corrugated iron church. The most prominent surviving building from the mining settlement is Beulah Chapel.

Ralegh's Cross was said to have been built originally as a landmark for travellers near a dangerous bog, north of the Brendon ridgeway. It is first documented in 1425/6, when it probably marked the boundary of the Ralegh estate at Nettlecombe (page 126).

124 *Beulah Chapel was opened in 1861 but the mines closed down in 1878-9 and the mining families moved away, resulting in the chapel closing in 1889. However, in 1907, mining resumed and the railway reopened for mineral and passenger traffic. The chapel was restored and reopened in 1910 and has stayed open, despite the mines closing once more.[1]*

124 *Originally to the north of what is now the B3190 road, the base of Ralegh's Cross was moved to its present position in the late eighteenth/early nineteenth century.*

125 *East from Ralegh's Cross, the intriguingly named 'Galloping Bottom Lane' leads to Windwhistle Lane and Windwhistle Barn, a nineteenth-century threshing barn.*

126 *The ridge to the south of Bird's Hill is extensively planted with blocks of conifers and deciduous trees.*

126 and 127 **Bird's Hill and Elworthy**

Elworthy is the easternmost settlement in Exmoor National Park. Mentioned in the Domesday Book of 1086 as Elwrde, meaning 'the old enclosure'.[4]

127 *St Martin's church, Elworthy, is thirteenth century with a fifteenth-century porch and nave roof. It was partly rebuilt in 1695 and 1846, and has been redundant since 1979.*

127 *The churchyard at Elworthy is marked by its ancient yew tree. An eighteenth-century chest tomb at the base of the tree is gradually being engulfed as the tree grows.*

J09 and J10 Heasley Mill and South Radworthy

The former Bampfylde mines lie in the valley to the north of Heasley Mill. Documentary evidence suggests that copper was being mined here from the fourteenth century. Intense activity began at the end of the 1600s and, by 1724, workings existed on either side of the valley. Work ceased at some time in the 1770s but the mine was re-opened in 1803-4. The nineteenth century saw a continuing exploitation of the workings by various companies. By mid-century, an attempt was made to work the gold deposits within the copper lodes, but it proved uneconomic. The 1870s saw an increase in iron production and a corresponding fall in the levels of copper production. Copper production appears to have ceased altogether in 1880, and the North Devon Mining Company was finally closed in 1885.[1]

J09 *Heasley House is thought to have been built in the mid-nineteenth century as the mine manager's (or captain's) house for the Bampfylde mine.*

J10 *Tabor Hill to the east of South Radworthy. The large fields are typical of mid-nineteenth century enclosures. Barcombe Down and North Molton Ridge to the top right remain unimproved.*

[Above] **J11** *North Molton Ridge with a fine display of flowering heather in August.*

J12 *Sandyway refers to a sandy or unsurfaced track. A shepherd's cottage here was converted to the Sportsman's Inn in 1840.[4]*

J11 *Darlick Moors lie to the north of North Molton Ridge. The area was known as Darlake in 1651, or dark lake.[4]*

J13 and J14 Twitchen Barrows and Tudball's Splats

J13 *Twitchen Barrows is a pair of Bronze Age barrows on Twitchen Ridge. While they are still prominent, both have been damaged in the past.*

Dane's Brook lies to the north side of Molland Moor. Dane's Brook was usually written 'Dun's Brook' before 1800, meaning 'stream from the hills'.[4] The brook provides the boundary between Devon and Somerset from Upper Willingford Bridge to its confluence with the River Barle, at which point the boundary heads south.

Four small enclosures in the heart of Withypool Common are mysteriously known as Tudball's Splats. The enclosures are still separately owned from the common, although they are being allowed to revert back to moorland.

J14 *Tudball Splats with Withypool Hill in the background.*

J13 *The small bridge at Lower Willingford provides a picturesque location.*

J14 and J15 **Porchester's Post and Barle Valley**

Porchester's Post is on the southern boundary of Withypool Common at Worthy Hill. A plaque on it reads: *"First erected in 1796 to mark the boundary of the Carnarvon Estate. Re-erected in memory of Lord Porchester, Earl of Carnarvon, the Chairman of the 1977 inquiry into the protection of moorland on Exmoor and to commemorate the Golden Jubilee of Queen Elizabeth II in 2002."*

Prior to 1796, Withypool Common formed part of the Pixton estate in Dulverton. Pixton belonged to the Acland family along with other estates at Holnicote and Killerton. In 1796, Elizabeth "Kitty" Acland married Henry George Herbert, 2nd Earl of Carnarvon and known by his courtesy title of Lord Porchester. They were given Pixton Park near Dulverton as part of her marriage settlement. That was when the estate become known as the Carnarvon estate as commemorated in the first part of the inscription.

The Exmoor estates remained with the Earls of Carnarvon (and Lords Porchester) until George Herbert, 5th Earl of Carnarvon (1866-1923) sold Pixton to his step-mother. George

Herbert is famous as an amateur Egyptologist who sponsored excavations by Howard Carter that discovered the tomb of Tutankhamun.

The middle part of the inscription on Porchester's Post refers to the time when the family connection with Exmoor was re-established in 1977. At that time, Henry Herbert (1924-2001), the then Lord Porchester (later the 7th Earl of Carnarvon), chaired a public inquiry to examine the loss of moorland on Exmoor due to ploughing (see page 51). His report proposed Moorland Conservation Orders, which would give the National Park Authority power to prevent farmers from ploughing up moorland if voluntary agreements could not be reached. In that event, financial compensation would be paid to the landowner. However, the Labour government's Countryside Bill of 1978, which included many of the recommendations of the Porchester Report, was not passed by the time of the 1979 General Election, which they lost to the Conservatives. The Conservative government introduced their own legislation, which became the Wildlife and Countryside Act 1981. Under the terms of this Act, management agreements with financial compensation for farmers and landowners were to be voluntary.[16]

J14 *Porchester's Post.*

J15 *The wooded slopes of the Barle valley characterise the landscape between Withypool and Tarr Steps.*

J16 Tarr Steps

Tarr Steps is a 58 metre long clapper bridge of 17 spans across the River Barle. The date of the bridge is a matter of debate. A prehistoric date has been proposed, but the account of the 1279 Perambulation of the moor crossed the River Barle at Three Waters about a mile to the south of Tarr Steps, which suggests that there was not a bridge here at that date.

A study in 2013 concluded that Tarr Steps was built in the fifteenth or sixteenth century to provide a dry way across the river alongside a long-established ford. The bridge would have provided access to a water-powered grist mill, sited close to the Barle on the Hawkridge side of the river. A leat over 1.5km long, which can still be seen in North Barton Wood, channelled water from West Water to drive the water wheel at the mill.

J16 *Despite the size of the stones, some of which weigh more than a tonne, Tarr Steps can suffer damage in severe floods, particularly when trees get swept downstream in the floodwater. A severe flood on 22 December 2012 dislodged a large section of the Steps. To facilitate the reconstruction after damage, the individual stones are numbered so that they can be replaced in their original positions.*

J16 *The impressive clapper bridge at Tarr Steps.*

J17 Winsford Hill

J17 *An impressive beech hedge on the south eastern boundary of Winsford Hill near Mounsey Hill Gate.*

[Left] **J17** *The Caratacus Stone lies on the south-eastern edge of Winsford Hill on the edge of a series of trackways associated with medieval and post medieval routes across Winsford Hill. An inscription was discovered in 1890 on the eastern face of the stone. It is in debased Latin writing of sixth century date, with letters about 9 centimetres high. It reads "CARAACI NEPVS" with the N reversed. This means either the grandson, nephew or descendent of Caratacus.[1] The stone is first documented in 1219.*

J17 *The shelter around the stone was erected in 1906 and affords some protection, but the stone is now badly weathered so that the inscription is very difficult to make out.*

J18 Edbrooke Hill

To the south of Winsford, the River Exe turns eastwards around the high ground of Edbrooke Hill. Edbrooke means 'head of the stream' and several small streams arise on all sides of the hill.

J18 *View from Edbrooke Hill northwards to Dunkery.*

J19 Bridgetown

J19 *Bridgetown is a small village close to Exton in the Exe valley south from Winsford.*

J19 *The cricket ground south of Bridgetown is reached via a footbridge over the River Exe. Its picturesque setting and unique thatched pavilion led to the ground winning the prize for Wisden's Loveliest Cricket Ground in 2002.*

[Right] **J19** *The occasional 'six' can lead to a fishing expedition in the Exe. Luckily, cricket balls float!.*

J20 Pulham Valley

Pulham means 'enclosure by the pool'. The Pulham River rises near Heath Poult Cross (Heath Poult is West Somerset dialect for the Black Grouse, a heathland bird that became extinct on Exmoor in the 1970s) and runs southwards to join the River Haddeo just below the dam of Wimbleball Reservoir **(K21)**.

J20 *View along Pulham Valley upstream from Brompton Regis (page 163).*

J21 and J22 **Hurscombe and Withiel Florey**

In 904, King Edward (The Elder) made a present of all his manors surrounding Taunton to the Bishop of Winchester. Withiel (meaning withy or willow) was part of this gift. The Bishop administered the estates via the monastery of Taunton. When, in 1100, William the Conqueror confirmed the donation, Winchester continued to own the lands and Taunton Priory to run them. The Augustinian canons of the Priory were almost certainly responsible for the first stone church at Withiel and its dedication to St Mary Magdalene is the same as that of the principal church of Taunton. The Priory sub-let its holdings to lay tenants and Ranulph de Flury is recorded as holding the Nynehead Florey and Withiel manors in 1237, with the family name remaining the name of the settlement to this day.[22]

J22 *The landscape at Withiel Florey.*

J22 *The impressive ruins south west of Withiel Florey are, in fact, remains of 'Blagdon Cottages', two semi-detached nineteenth century farm workers' cottages. The two, 2-roomed, 2-storey cottages had semi-circular bays or "bastions" projecting eastwards and overlooking the river valley. It is probable that the cottages were built in this style to give a castellated appearance when viewed from Withiel Florey, where a mansion had existed for a short time in the early 1800s.[1]*

J22 *St Mary Magdalene's church in Withiel Florey has an early foundation as in 1110 the living was appropriated to Taunton Priory. The west tower is thirteenth century but the rest of the building is fifteenth century with later restoration.[1]*

[Facing page] **J21** *The valley at Hurscombe is now flooded by the northern arm of Wimbleball Reservoir which was constructed in the 1970s (see* **K21**).

J23 Beverton Pond source of the River Tone

Beverton Pond lies on the eastern boundary of the National Park around 2 kilometres west of Ralegh's Cross. It is considered to be the source of the River Tone, a Celtic river name possibly meaning 'roaring stream'. Taunton gets its name from a combination of Tone and the Old English tun for 'enclosure' or 'settlement', i.e. Tone Tun.

J23 *After a dry summer there is a grassy hollow where the pond should be!*

J23 *A more impressive pond in winter.*

K10 and K11 **Brinsworthy and Holywell**

Brinsworthy is 'Bryni's settlement', Bruneswrthi in 1238. The farm at Brinsworthy is said to have been originally a medieval three-room plan building.

K10 *A barn at Brinsworthy Farm, part stone and part cob in construction. Cob was a common building material in Devon and Cornwall and was made by combining clay-based subsoil with sand, straw and water mixed and trampled using oxen. Cob building deserves to be revived, cob is readily available, cheap, versatile and very stable when protected from the weather.*

K11 *Lane at Holywell Bridge – not much to see by way of a well or a bridge!*

North east of Brinsworthy, the site of a holy well is marked on the modern Ordnance Survey 1:25,000 map around 400 metres south of Holywell Bridge. Unfortunately, little can be seen of the former well that is thought to have been medieval in origin. The well was ascribed curative powers associated with the eyes, and throughout the nineteenth century and up to the First World War was visited by pilgrims on Maundy Thursday and Ascension Day.

> *"Holy Well Revels were held annually on Ascension Day, when in the only flat field below the spring, a fair was held, together with sports and dancing. Many talls were erected, shooting galleries and swing boats...".[1]*

K11 *The housing for water filters installed below Holywell Reservoir in 1913 to supply water to South Molton.*

K12 *View of the hamlet at Twitchen from Cussacombe Common.*

K12 **Twitchen**

The name Twitchen is a common place name in North Devon. Several derivations of the name are suggested including that it comes from the Old English 'twicene' meaning crossways; or means two valleys; or the land between two streams; or land covered with rough herbage such as twitch grass. All the options seem possible in the case of this Twitchen.

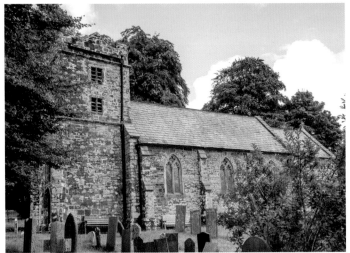

> K12 *A church is first mentioned on this site in Twitchen in 1340. The tower is of fifteenth-century origin, but the rest of the church was rebuilt and the tower altered in 1844. The font dates from the twelfth century but was also restored.[1]*

K13 Cussacombe Post

K13 *The Cussacombe Post. A plaque on the post states, "The original post was erected to commemorate The Diamond Jubilee of Queen Victoria in 1897. A replacement post was erected to commemorate The Silver Jubilee of Queen Elizabeth II in 1977. This plaque was installed to commemorate the Diamond Jubilee of Queen Elizabeth II in 2012."*

K14 *Much of the Dane's Brook valley was improved for farming in the early 1800s. This view from Brimblecombe Hill shows Cloggs Farm with Cloggs Down to the middle left and Old Barrow Down on the horizon. Although the two Downs are covered in seminatural vegetation today, the traces of field boundaries can be seen from aerial photographs showing that attempts at cultivation were more extensive in the past.*

K14 and K15 **Dane's Brook Valley**

K15 *Hawkridge Cross is alternatively known as Mare Pool Cross named after a small quarry nearby which presumably contained a pond, although it is now filled in.*

K14 *Dane's Brook below Lower Willingford Bridge.*

K16 and K17 **Hawkridge and Mounsey Hill**

K16 *South from Tarr Steps the River Barle meanders south west and then turns south east below Hawkridge Ridge.*

Mounsey Hill lies across the Barle valley from Hawkridge. On its southern slopes, Ashwick House was built in 1901 by a businessman, Heber Mardon, who was head of Mardon, Son & Hall, a printing business in Bristol famous for producing picture cards for cigarettes produced by W.D. & H.O. Wills, also based in Bristol.

K16 *The small settlement of Hawkridge sits, as its name suggests, high on the ridge itself. St Giles parish church in Hawkridge has a Norman south door and a chancel and base of tower dating to the fourteenth century. It was restored in 1878. There is a Norman font inside and an intriguing medieval tomb slab that might have covered the grave of the warden of Exmoor Royal Forest, William de Plessy, who died in 1274.[25] The remains of a medieval cross survive in the churchyard.*

K17 *In 1928, Frank Green purchased Ashwick House and surrounding estate. In those days 20 resident staff ran the*

house and, to provide for entertainment of the staff, a miniature theatre (sometimes known as the music room) was constructed in the grounds.

K17 *The music room was restored by the Moorland Mousie Trust, a charity based at Ashwick that helps to conserve the Exmoor pony. The name of the charity comes from a story written in 1929, about the life of an Exmoor pony called Mousie.*

K18 and K19 Broford and Chilly Bridge

K19 *Broford Wood occupies steep ground on the western side of the Exe valley south of Bridgetown.*

K19 *The house at Chilly Bridge was originally a tollhouse on the turnpike road between Minehead and Exebridge – now the A396 (see page 92). The intriguing name 'Chilly' might mean 'bridge by a small clearing', from the Old English 'cild' for child and 'ley' for grassy area.[4] The bridge is eighteenth century or earlier, restored in the late nineteenth century.*

K18 *View from Halscombe looking east. Halscombe means valley where hazel grows from the West Somerset dialect 'halse' for hazel.[4]*

K20 Brompton Regis

Before the Norman Conquest, the manor was held by Gytha Thorkelsdóttir, a Danish noble woman and mother of Harold Godwinson, the Harold that lost to William at the Battle of Hastings in 1066.[2]

After the battle, the manor was seized by William the Conqueror, leading to it being known as King's Brompton, or, Brunetone as it is named in the Domesday Book.[22]

K20 *The tower at St Mary's church in Brompton Regis is thirteenth century. [Right] The organ in the south transept is said to be by T.C. Lewis who built it in London in 1872 for "a gentleman" whose identity remains unknown, and who returned it 24 years later in part exchange for an even more powerful instrument. After an overhaul, it came to Brompton Regis through a fund-raising effort by the parishioners, as their chosen way of commemorating the Diamond Jubilee of Queen Victoria in 1897. It was cleaned and restored in 2012.*[22]

K21 and K22 **Wimbleball Lake**

In the late 1960s proposals for a water supply reservoir on Exmoor came from the Devon River Authority (which included part of West Somerset). The authority was seeking to construct a 'regulating' reservoir to supply the anticipated needs of three water boards (West Somerset, East Devon and North Devon). By 1969, the search had narrowed to two possible Exmoor sites – Landacre and the Haddeo valley.

The Landacre site proposed a dam about 800 metres downstream of Landacre Bridge. If it had been built there, the water would have submerged the bridge and extended up the Barle to near Wheal Eliza (see **G12**). Cow Castle **(H12)** would have become an island. In its favour, the dam at Landacre would have held more water than the Haddeo site, cost less to construct and inundate no houses.

The Haddeo scheme would require a higher dam but was regarded as having less landscape impact. Also, the site would allow pumping of water to supplement the supply at Clatworthy Reservoir to the east.

Ultimately, the Haddeo valley was chosen and work commenced in 1974 and was completed in October 1978. Today, the 49 metre (161 feet) high dam provides a water storage capacity of some 21,000 million litres over an area of 1.51 km^2 (374 acres).

During periods of low flow in the River Exe, additional water is released from the base of the dam to augment the flow of the Haddeo River and replenish the Exe so that it can be extracted at Bolham near Tiverton to supply drinking water without depleting the river overall. When the reservoir is low, and when there is sufficient water in the River Exe, three pumps located at Exebridge are used to pump water from the Exe up to the reservoir so that it can be stored and released back to the river when needed.

K21 Wimbleball Lake from near Lyddon's Cottages on the eastern bank of the reservoir.

L13 and L14 Molland Moor and Brimblecombe Hill

L13 *Smallacombe Combe is one of a series of small combes that contain streams draining the south of Molland Moor.*

L14 *Anstey Combe is another. Stream gulley erosion in Anstey Combe (named Anstey's Gully on current Ordnance Survey maps) revealed a sequence of unusually deep alternating silt and gravel deposits that reached depths of almost 6 metres in comparison to similar deposits in neighbouring combes that do not exceed 1-2 metres. The sediments have been geomorphologically sampled and dated to the Roman period and sixteenth-seventeenth centuries AD. Given the small catchment area of the combe, comparable to that of the neighbouring valleys, the two unusually thick sediment deposits may indicate episodes of high sediment supply to the valley floor, suggesting periods of iron mining in these periods within Anstey Combe.[1]*

L14 *Close to the road on the eastern side of Brimblecombe Hill, the Froude Stone provides a memorial to Philip Froude Hancock who was the fifth son of William Hancock, a Wiveliscombe brewer and banker. Philip Froude played rugby for Somerset and England and became a huntsman on Exmoor. He died in 1933 and the stone memorial was brought to this site in 1935.[1]*

L15 **West Anstey Common**

L15 *The sculpture near Badlake Moor Cross is close to the point where the Two Moors' Way long-distance footpath enters the Exmoor National Park. The sculpture was created by Peter Randall-Page in 2004 by cutting a granite boulder in half so that each cut face is a mirror image of the other. The other half of the boulder is sited 30 miles to the south, close to the point where the Two Moors' Way leaves the Dartmoor National Park.*

L15 *View along the Ridge Road that crosses West Anstey Common. Anstey is thought to mean 'narrow path' from Old English 'an' meaning one and 'stigel' meaning path.*

L15 *North of the Ridge Road, the West Anstey Barrows are prominent features, although they have suffered from damage in the past.*

L16 East Anstey Common

L16 *Large beech hedge at Whiterocks Down.*

L16 *Whiterocks Down lies to the north of East Anstey Common.*

L16 *View north from Venford Moor. 'Ven' means 'fen' or marshy ground. The moorland at Ashway Side is visible on the horizon.*

L17 and L18 River Barle, Marsh Bridge, Dulverton Weir and Oldberry Castle

The River Barle flows eastwards to Marsh Bridge where it turns south before taking a wide meander around the promontory of Burridge Woods which has Oldberry (or Oldbury) Castle at its summit. 'Bury' and 'Berry' derive from the Old English 'burgh' meaning fortification and several fortification locations on Exmoor have this name, including Bury itself (page 174). The name for Burridge Woods presumably derives from having a fortification on a ridge.

Beyond the promontory, the river heads south again towards Dulverton where a large weir serves to direct water towards the town. Recent investigations indicate that the weir is one of the best-preserved medieval weirs in England and is built using an oak 'stake-and-boulder' technology, first introduced by the Normans and used throughout the medieval period.

A number of oak stakes were recovered from the weir in 2014 following flood damage and some of these were subsequently analysed using tree ring dating (dendrochronology). Two stakes appeared to have been sourced from a tree felled in around 1784 and a group of stakes have felling dates between 1801 and 1803, suggesting two phases of repair.[1] These stakes are unlikely to be as old as the weir itself, as weirs are frequently damaged by floods and the 'stake and boulder' construction method is readily reparable using locally available materials.

L18 *The weir at Dulverton is likely to have been first constructed sometime before 1331 when there is the first mention of a mill in the area. The Dulverton Weir and Leat Conservation Trust was established in 2016 to restore the weir and the leat system that supplied water to mills in the town.[23]*

L18 *Marsh Bridge is probably eighteenth century. It was repaired in 1818-9 and altered in 1866-7 when the central pier was removed and an iron bridge inserted. The parapet was destroyed in the major flood of 1952 and reconstructed in steel in 1979-80.[1]*

L18 *Part of the embankment of Oldberry Castle, an Iron Age hillfort. The north-east part of the defences survives well in woodland, but the rest is incorporated in massive hedge banks and the interior is under cultivation.[1]*

[Facing page] **L17** *The steep valley slopes along the River Barle provide a nearly unbroken woodland cover from south of Withypool to Dulverton.*

L19 and L20 Barlynch and River Haddeo

Above Helebridge, the River Exe flows southwards through a steep sided valley that provides a corridor for the former toll road from Helebridge to Dunster (now A396) (see page 92 for more on the toll road). At Barlynch, the valley floor widens and this was the location of the medieval Priory of St Nicholas, a branch of Cleeve Abbey near Washford. The priory was founded in around 1174 and dissolved around 1537 during the Dissolution of the Monasteries by Henry VIII.

L19 *Barlynch Farm House is probably mainly seventeenth and eighteenth century and is built on the site of the former priory. Little remains of the priory apart from some ruins in the grounds of the house.*

The track through Brockhole Wood heads east to a ridge running parallel to the Exe valley. Continuing east, the land descends into the valley of the River Haddeo. The upper reaches of the Haddeo were dammed for Wimbleball Reservoir in the 1970s **(K21)** and the lower river receives its water from the reservoir and from the River Pulham **(J20)** that joins the river below the dam at Hartford.

L19 *Brockhole Wood is on the slopes above Barlynch. The byway through the wood is lined by beech trees including this particularly large example.*

L20 *River Haddeo below Hartford.*

L21 Haddon Hill

L21 *Haddon Hill is a high ridge of Devonian Pickwell Down Sandstone to the south of the National Park. It forms the largest remaining area of heathland in the eastern part of Exmoor and provides an excellent vantage point to see Wimbleball Lake to the north.*

L22 Upton

[Left, top and bottom] **L22** *The remains of the fourteenth-century former St James church, Upton, are alongside Upton Farm. Today, only the west tower and the lowest courses of the nave and chancel survive. In the 1860s, the church was considered to be too far from the village and a new one was built in 1870 in the main settlement. The nave and chancel of the old church were pulled down in 1891 and the tower was made safe in 1973.[1] The bells from the church have been reused elsewhere, including one at the St John the Baptist in Pitney, Somerset, and one in Green Point, New South Wales, Australia.[2]*

The original settlement of Upton was clustered around the former parish church of St James at Upton Farm, while a settlement by the main road used to be named Whitley. When a new church was provided in 1870 on a new location on the main road, people going to the new church started to call the houses on the main road Upton and this replaced the name of Whitley.

L22 *Haddon Lodge, or the 'Pepperpot Castle', is at the eastern end of Haddon Hill above Upton Cleave. It was built in the early nineteenth century as a lodge to Lady Harriett's Drive. The drive was built by Lady Harriet Acland during the long period of her widowhood, 1778-1815, to connect Pixton Park at Dulverton (where her daughter the Countess of Carnarvon lived) with her own estates near Wiveliscombe.[1]*

M18 **Dulverton**

Dulverton is 'Dulvertune' in the Domesday Book in 1086 when the manor was owned by the King. In 1306, a market and three day fair were granted and, in 1340, the town was granted to the Augustinian priory at Taunton. At the Dissolution of the Monasteries in the 1540s, possession reverted to the King. Under Philip and Mary, control of Dulverton's affairs was handed to ten local citizens, one of whom, a Sydenham, purchased the manor in 1568. The presence of six mills, recorded in 1568, suggests an active woollen industry which it seems continued until at least the early part of the nineteenth century – see **L18**.

M18 *Dulverton Bridge over the River Barle is medieval in origin. It was repaired in 1624, subsequently widened by 5 feet (1.5 metres) on the upstream side in 1819, and repaired in 1866 and 1952-3 after flood damage.[1]*

M18 *The Town Hall or Market House is now a hall over shops. In 1760, it was agreed that a Market House would be built to replace the Shambles, but it was to be more than 100 years before they were demolished and the current building erected in 1866. The lower floor of the Market House was used mainly for market stalls and the upper room was used for functions, including the Magistrates Court. It was converted with the addition of external steps in 1927. During the Second World War, evacuated school children were taught at the Town Hall, and the Town Hall kitchen was used to cook food for the schools.[1]*

Exmoor House was built in 1854 as the Dulverton Workhouse. It was built in a T-shaped plan, with separate accommodation for males and females. Before 1834, poor people were looked after by providing food and clothing bought with money collected from land owners and other wealthy people in the local parish. The Poor Law Amendment Act of 1834, ensured that no able-bodied person could get poor relief unless they went to live in special workhouses. Workhouses also housed orphaned and abandoned children, the physically and mentally sick, the disabled, the elderly and unmarried mothers.

In the earliest days, the government was terrified of encouraging 'idlers' and made sure that people feared the workhouse and would do anything to avoid having to live in one. Families were split up and residents were made to wear a uniform so that everyone outside knew they were poor and lived in the workhouse. The food was tasteless and was the same day after day, and residents were made to work hard, often doing unpleasant jobs. Later, the emphasis changed to rehabilitation of residents to enable them to become independent and to provide a refuge for those most in need in the parish.

M18 *Today, after many other uses, the former workhouse building is used as offices by the Exmoor National Park Authority.*

M19 and M20 **Bury**

Bury probably takes its name from the fortification above the settlement at the end of a high ridge running north and south above the junctions of the River Exe with its tributary the Haddeo.

*M19 There is no documentation relating to Bury Castle but it is believed that the site is a reused iron age enclosure with a motte added sometime in the eleventh or twelfth centuries to form a small 'motte-and-bailey' structure (see **D06**).[1]*

M20 *The medieval packhorse bridge over the River Haddeo at Bury is on the line of an ancient road called Fort Lane.*

N19 Meeting of the Waters

Perry Farm on the southern slopes of Pixton Hill is at the southernmost part of Exmoor National Park. The River Barle and River Exe run on either side of Pixton Hill and come together about 600 metres south of Perry Farm.

Although the Exe is the dominant name for the catchment, the River Barle is the larger river at the confluence.

N19 *River Exe to the east of Perry Farm, shortly after it has left the National Park.*

N19 *River Barle to the west of Perry Farm where it leaves the National Park.*

N19 *Looking south at the confluence of the River Exe (on the left) and the River Barle (on the right). (The site is only accessible with permission as the location is on private land.)*

References and Further Reading

Much of the research for this book has been undertaken using authoritative sources that are accessible on the internet.

1 – The Exmoor Historic Environment Record (HER) www.exmoorher.co.uk/home is a web-based resource that has been compiled by Exmoor National Park Authority and provides archaeological and historical information for land, buildings and monuments across Exmoor. The HER has been the source or starting point for discovering much of the historical information in this book.

2 – Wikipedia is a free online encyclopedia with information on a very wide range of topics. The articles are authored by knowledgeable volunteers and are mostly referenced enabling statements to be checked.

More specific sources include:

3 – Edwards R.A., *Exmoor Geology*, 2000, Exmoor Books

4 – Allen, N.V., *Exmoor Place Names*, 1991, Alcombe Books

5 – MacEwan, A. & MacEwan, M., *National Parks: conservation or cosmetics?* 1982, Allen & Unwin

6 – Binding, H. & Pearce, B., *Exmoor Village – Celebrating the Enduring Landscape of Exmoor and its People Over Fifty Years*, 2004, Exmoor Books. Includes the full text of *Exmoor Village* by W.J. Turner published in 1947.

7 – Yalden, D., *The History of British Mammals*, 1999, Poyser.

8 – Hegarty, C., & Wilson-North, R., *The Archaeology of Hill Farming on Exmoor*, 2014, English Heritage

9 – Allen, N.V., T*he Waters of Exmoor*, 1978, Exmoor Press

10 – Friends of Hoar Oak http://hoaroakcottage.org/

11 – Exmoor Mires Partnership http://www.exmoormires.org.uk

12 – Burton, R.A., *The Heritage of Exmoor*, p. 120-1 (Monograph). 1989, SEM7230.

13 – Allen, N, *Exmoor's Wild Red Deer,* 1990, Exmoor Press

14 – Easterbrook, M., *Butterflies of Britain and Ireland – A Field and Site Guide*, 2010, A&C Black

15 – Turnpike Roads of England and Wales website http://www.turnpikes.org.uk

16 – Off the beaten track in Somerset is an online blog that has well-researched articles on hidden away and unusual locations across the county, http://offthebeatentrackinsomerset.blogspot.com/

17 – Website for the Devon Closewool Sheep Association http://devonclosewool.com/about-the-breed/

18 – Website for the Exmoor Pony Society http://www.exmoorponysociety.org.uk/

19 – Website for the Rare Breeds Survival Trust https://www.rbst.org.uk/Pages/Category/equine-watchlist

20 – Exmoor National Park Authority, 2010, *A Field Guide to Exmoor's Early Iron Industry*

21 – Website with the history and archaeology of the West Somerset Mineral Railway and associated mine workings on the Brendon Hills http://www.westsomersetmineralrailway.org.uk

22 – Website for Brompton Regis parish http://bromptonregis.com/

23 – Website for the Dulverton Weir and Leat Trust http://dulvertonweir.org.uk/

24 – http://www.exmoor-nationalpark.gov.uk/Whats-Special/culture/literary-links/ada-lovelace

25 – Eardley-Wilmot, H., *Yesterday's Exmoor*, 1990, Exmoor Books

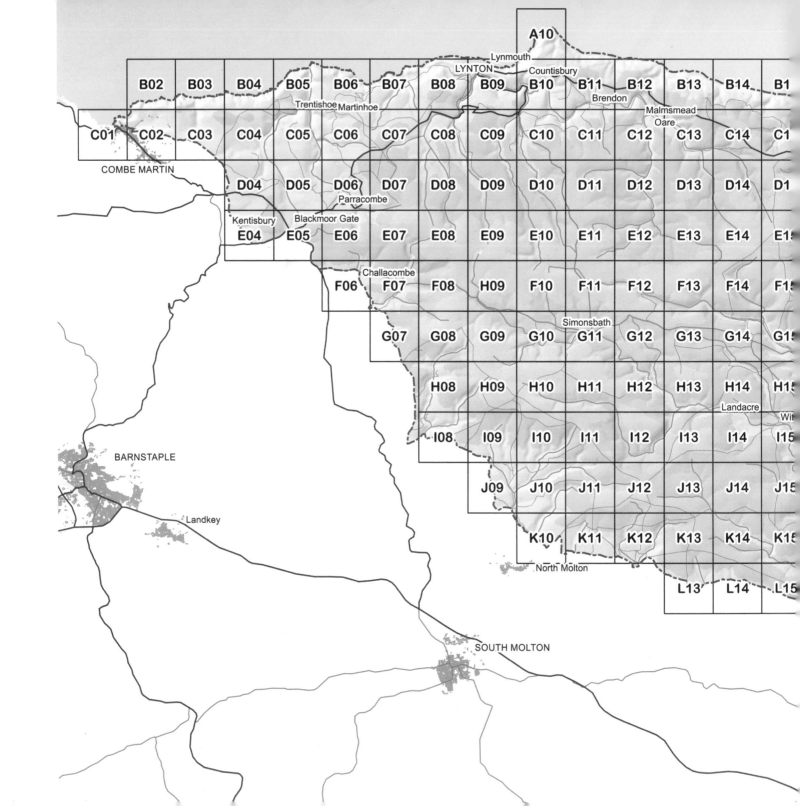